دعنا نتحدث بالعربية

LET US CONVERSE IN

ARABIC

Also by the same author in UBSPD

Arabic for Beginners

دعنا نتحدث بالعربية

LET US CONVERSE IN
ARABIC

Dr. SYED ALI

HIPPOCRENE BOOKS, INC.
171 Madison Avenue
New York, NY 10016

For information, address :
HIPPOCRENE BOOKS, INC.
171 Madison Avenue
New York, NY 10016

Published in arrangement with
UBS Publishers' Distributors Ltd.
5 Ansari Road, New Delhi-110 002 (India)

Printed in India.

CONTENTS

INTRODUCTION

Arabic is one of the widely spoken languages of the world like English and French. It is of ancient origin and prose and poetical compositions of the remote past have been codified and preserved by anthologists of the medieval period. These works are still popular with people of the area and Arabic scholars as they throw light on the history, culture, manners and customs of the people in the pre-Islamic era. Arabic language, which was once confined to the Hejaz in the Arabian peninsula has, after the dawn of Islam, rapidly advanced towards the East and the West. The purity of the language has been preserved with a rare sense of dedication throughout its steady progress in foreign lands. During the last fourteen centuries, Eastern and Western languages were enriched by its vocabulary as Arabic was the language of science, medicine and learned thought during the early stages of human civilization. However in recent times, taking into consideration the phenomenal growth of science and technology, words of foreign origin have crept into Arabic dictionaries due to sheer necessity.

Arabic is now spoken over a vast area comprising various continents. It is the official language of nearly twenty-five sovereign states and one of the recognised languages of international organisations. The morphology and syntax of written Arabic are essentially the same all over the Arab world. The language of the print media, official communication and text books is based on the Quranic language. This has been used as a means to ensure common cultural heritage and linguistic unity of the Arabs. Colloquial Arabic is merely a dialect with a weaker grammatical base, the Arabs of each area speak the language with a distinct local accent. Though understood within the larger Arab community, the non-Arabs find it difficult to follow, hence the need to learn widely acceptable form of expression.

The object of writing this book is to enable the non-Arabs in the Arab situation to communicate with the people there and convey their immediate requirements. Visitors to the Arab Gulf states for the purpose of tourism, trade, employment or residence are delighted to listen to Arabic conversation, radio and T.V programmes. They develop a natural liking for the language and aspire to develop the ability to converse in Arabic not only for the sheer delight that it provides but to feel at home

with the local population. Pronunciation of certain Arabic letters could pose a problem but by constant practice and listening to radio programmes or direct contacts with the Arabs one can gain confidence. Transliteration, as found in this volume, could be of help to a certain extent only. There is no alternative to learning any language except through reading and writing.

4, Begum Sahib Street,
Royapettah, Madras,
India

SYED ALI

ARABIC ALPHABET

The Arabic alphabet is written here with their equivalent symbols in English as used in this volume.

Arabic letter	Name in in Arabic	Symbols used in this book	Examples in English
أ	hamzah	a	abide (a)
ا	alif	ā	
ب	ba	b	book (b)
ت*	ta	t	eighth (t)
ث	tha	ṯ	mouth (th)
ج	jim	j	jam (j)
ح	ha	ḥ	heavy (h)
خ	ka	ḵ	khan (kh)
د	dal	d	width (d)
ذ	dal	ḏ	this (is)
ر	ra	r	charm (r)
ز	zay	z	zeel (z)
س	sin	s	sin (s)
ش	shin	sh	shop (sh)
ص	sad	ṣ	soft (s)

* ة when used at the end of a feminine noun or adjective.

ض	dad	ḍ	Ramadan (d) it is an emphatic d and peculiar to Arabic language
ط	ta	ṭ	a slight variation of the sound ت
ظ	za	ẓ	a slight variation of the sound ذ
ع	ayn	'a	it is a voiced correlative of "أ"
غ	gain	ḡ	it is a voiced correlative of خ
ف	fa	f	force (f)
ق	qaf	q	question (q)
ك	kaf	k	kind (k)
ل	lam	l	long (l)
م	mim	m	mint (m)
ن	nun	n	noun (n)
هـ*	ha	h	host (h)
و	waw	w	wide (w)
ي	ya	y	young (y)

Arabic alphabet consist of twenty eight letters which are written from the right to left. All the twenty eight letters are consonants. Three of these letters الف, و , ي are used as long vowels.

* ه when used at the end of a word

دعـنـا نـتـحـدث بـالعربيـة

LET US CONVERSE IN ARABIC

da'nā nataḥaddaṯ bi al 'arabiya — دعـنـا نـتـحـدث بـالعربيـة

Let us converse in Arabic

hada ṣa'bun lī — هـذا صـعـب لي

This is difficult for me

bal basīṭ iḏ ladaika raḡba — بـل بسـيـط إذ لديك رغبـة

But it is easy, if you wish.

lā a'arifu al qira'a wa al kitāba — لا أعرف القـراءة والكتـابـة

I don't know reading and writing

hiya luḡa qadīma — هـي لـغـة قـديـمـة

It is an ancient language

wa al luḡa al-rasmia fi al 'alam al 'arabī

واللغة الرسمية في العالم العربي

It is an official language in the Arab world.

al 'arab fataḥū ma'ahid li tadrīsiha — العرب فتحوا معاهد لتدريسها

The Arabs have opened institutes for teaching it.

al-durūs tuḏā'a bi al-rādio — الـدروس تـذاع بـالـراديو

Lessons are broadcast over the radio

wal kutub lil mubtadīn kaṯira — والكتـب لـلـمبـتـديـن كثيـرة

There are many books for beginners

nujarrib mukālama fi ba'ḍ al aḥyān — نـجرب مكالـمـة في بعض

fi al-sūq wa al maktab — الاحيـان في السـوق والمكتـب

We shall practice conversation
now and then in the market and office.

yalzam 'alaika al qira'a wa al kitāba يلزم عليك القراءة والكتابة

Reading and writing are essential for you.

haḏa yakuḏ waqt هـذا يـأخـذ وقتـا

This takes time

'aliyka an tatashawir ustaḏ عليك أن تتـشـاور اسـتـاذا

You should consult a teacher

aw durūs musajjala 'ala sharīt أو دروس مسجلـة علي شريـط

Or (consult) lessons recorded on tapes.

ḥawil wantahiz al furṣa حـاول وانتـهـز الفـرصـة

Try and make use of the opportunity.

muwaffaq insha Allah مـوفق إن شـاء اللـه

You will succeed, God willing.

VOCABULARY (GENERAL)

intihaz al furṣa انتهاز الفرصة
making use of opportunity
muwaffaq موفق
successful
muḥawala محاولة
effort
mustaḥīl مستحيل
impossible
mumkin ممكن
possible
musajjil مسجل
registrar
sharīṭ,musajjal شريط،مسجل
tape recorder
ma'had معهد
institute
aḥyān أحيان
some time
luḡa لغة
language
lisān لسان
tongue, language
ṣa'b صعب
difficult

iḏa'a إذاعة
broadcasting
maftūḥ مفتوح
opened
muḡlaq مغلق
locked, shut
wafra وفرة
plenty
tajriba تجربة
test, attempt
mukālama مكالمة
conversation
kalām كلام
speech
muḥadaṯa محادثة
conversation, discussion
ba'ḍ بعض
some
lāzim لازم
necessary
mashwara مشورة
consultation
mustashār مستشار
adviser

basīṭ بسيط
simple

'arafa عرف
to know

qirā'a قراءة
reading

kitāba كتابة
writing

ma'rifa معرفة
learning

ma'rūf معروف
recognised, good

qadīm قديم
old

rasmi رسمي
official

majāl مجال
scope, extent

tadrīs تدريس
teaching

dars درس
lesson

insha' Allah إن شاء الله
God willing

lada لدي
at, with, in

raḡba رغبة
desire

'ālam عالم
world, universe

'arabi عربي
Arab

mubtadi' مبتدي
beginner

māhir ماهر
experienced

mā sha' Allah ما شاء الله
God intended

mahāra مهارة
experience

ikbār إخبار
news

mu<u>k</u>ābara مخابرة
correspondence

murāsala مراسلة
correspondence

mursil مرسل
sender

لدي القنصليـــة

AT THE CONSULATE

urid al-safar ila jedda أريـد السفـر إلـي جــدة
I wish to travel to Jeddah

ana bi ḥāja ila ta'shīra al-duḵūl أنـا بحـاجـة إلي تأشيـرة الـدخـول
I am in need of Entry Visa

ḥaṣaltu 'ala taḏkira murāja'a حصلت علي تذكرة مراجعة
I have obtained visa advice memo.

ta'shīra ṣādira min wizāra تاشيرة صادرة من وزارة

al ḵārijiya al-saūdiya الخارجية السعودية
It was issued by Saudi Ministry of Foreign Affairs.

wa ladaia jawaz as-safar ولـدي جـواز السـفر
I have with me a passport.

ṣalaḥiya ta'shīra tantahi ba'da shahı

صلاحية التأشيرة تنتهي بعد شهر
Validity of the visa expires after a month.

al vakīl ṭalabani ila Bombay الوكـيـل طلبني إلي بومبي
The Agent called me to Bombay.

ṣaḥib al-sharika aiḍan maujud hunak

صـاحب الشركة أيضا موجود هناك
The owner of the company is also available there.

aḏhab ila al qunṣuliya al-saūdia أذهب إلي القنصليـة السعودية
I shall go to the Saudi consulate.

haḏihi al waṯā'iq al maṭlūba هـذه الوثـائق المطلوبة
These are the documents that are required

wa muṣaddaqa min jiha rasmiya ومصدقة من جهة رسمية

and these are endorsed by official authority.

al muwaẓẓaf fi al qunṣuliya الموظف في القنصلية يفحص

yafḥaṣ al awrāq wa yaṭlub ba'ḍ الأوراق ويطلب بعض المعلومات

al m'alūmāt 'an al wakīl. عن الوكيل

The officer in the consulate (scrutinise) verifies the papers and asks for some information about the agent.

raqm al-sijill al-tijāri min faḍlak رقم السجل التجاري من فضلك

Please (give) the commercial code No.

al ḥamdu lillahi ḥaṣaltu 'ala أحمد لله حصلت علي

ta'shīra al-dukūl تأشيرة الدخول

Praise be to God! I have obtained Entry Visa.

wa qabla ḏalika ḥaṣaltu 'ala وقبل ذلك حصلت علي

al-shahāda al-ṭibbiya الشهادة الطبية

And before that I had got Health Certificate.

ana ḏahib ila mudīr al jawazat أنا ذاهب الي مدير الجوازات

wa al hijra والهجرة

I am proceeding to the director of passports and immigration.

qaddamtu lahu tafāṣīl ḥaula 'aqd قدمت له تفاصيل حول عقد

al 'amal wa ma'lūmāt 'an al-ratib العمل ومعلومات عن الراتب

al-shahri الشهري

I have presented to him details about employment (contract),agreement and information about monthly salary.

wāfaqa mudīr al hijra — وافق مدير الهجرة

The Director of immigration approved.

ğadan saufa adhab ila maktab sharika al-ṭayrān — غدا سوف اذهب الي مكتب شركة الطيران

Tomorow I shall go to the Airline Office.

رحلـــة الـــي جـــدة

JOURNEY TO JEDDAH

ladaia tadkira al-safar ila Jeddah لدي تذكرة السفر الي جدة

I have with me travel ticket to Jeddah.

al maṭār muzdaḥim ألمطار مزدحم

The Airport is crowded.

istalamtu bitāqa al-dukūl ila al-ṭā'ira

استلمت بطاقة الدخول الي الطائرة

I have received boarding card (for the plane)

sullam al-ṭā'ira amāmi سلم الطائرة أمامي

The ladder of the plane is infront of me.

laisa li illa al murūr bi qism al amn ليس لي الا المرور بقسم الامن

I have now only to pass through security.

al muḍīfa: ahlan wa sahlan المضيفة : أهلا سهلا

The Airhostess: Welcome!

maq'ad raqm ṯalāṯa, min faḍlak مقعد رقم ٣ من فضلك.

Seat No. 3, please.

al-tadkīn mamnū' ألتدخين ممنوع

Smoking is prohibited.

al mudīfa ta'ti bi ṣīniya المضيفة تأتي بصينية

The Airhostess comes with a tray.

fiha al lauz wa baskawīt فيها اللوز وبسكويت

With almonds and biscuits in it.

al-shai min faḍlak الشاي من فضلك

Tea please.

ḥāḍir حاضـر
(It is) ready.
naḥnu qarīb min Jeddah نحن قريبا من جـدة
We are near(ing) Jeddah.
nanzil 'ala al maṭār ba'd نـنزل علي المطـار بـعد
ṯalaṯa daqā'iq ثـلاثـة دقائق
We will land at the airport after three minutes.
shukran lakum شكـرا لكـم
Thank you.
al-shanaṭ fi al gamārik الشنط في الجمارك
The luggage is in the customs.
al-shurṭi: hal usāiduka الشرطي: هل أساعدك
Police: Can I help you.
ana bi intiẓār mandūb al-sharika أنا بانتظار مندوب الشركة
I am waiting for the representative of the company.
al isti'lamāt min faḍlak الاستعلامات من فضلك
Information office, please.
ittaṣal bi al-sharika 'ala al-telephone اتصل بالشركة علي التلفون
Contact the company over the phone.
haḏa huwa, ahlan wa sahlan هذا هو : أهلا وسهلا
Here he is, Welcome.
kunnā bi intiẓārika كنا بانتظارك
We were waiting for you.
ana sa'īd bi liqā'ika أنا سعيد بلقائك
I am happy to meet you.
'ataqid anta t'abān أعتقد أنت تعبان
I suppose you are tired.

k̲ud̲ rāḥa خـذ راحـة

Take rest.

ana murīh أنـا مـريـح

I am comfortable.

al-sā'iq yak̲ud̲uka ila al funduq السـائـق يـأخذك الي الفنـدق

The driver will take you to the hotel.

al funduq qarīb min maktab al-sharika

الفندق قريب من مكتب الشركة

The hotel is near the company's office.

ta'āl ila al maktab ḡad تعـال الي المـكتـب غـدا

Come to the office tomorrow.

yakūn ma'ak jawāz al-safar يكـون معـك جـواز السفـر

The passport shall be with you.

had̲a ḍarūri li iṣdār al iqāma هذا ضروري لاصدار الاقامـة

This is necessary for the issue of Residence Permit.

DOCUMENTS : TRAVEL AND EMPLOYMENT

mut'ab	متعب	qunṣul	قنصـــل
tired		*consul*	
kafīl	كفيـل	qunṣuliya	قنصليـة
sponsor		*consulate*	
makfūl	مكفول	safīr	سـفير
person sponsored		*ambassador*	
taḏkira	تـذكـرة	sifāra	سـفارة
ticket		*embassy*	
maṭār	مـطار	wuṣūl	وصـول
airport		*arrival*	
jawaz al-safar	جواز	muḡādara	مغـادرة
passport		*departure*	
istiḵdām	إستخدام	qism al amn	قسـم الأمـن
employment		*security department*	
iqāma	إقامـة	al amn ai 'āmm	الأمـن العـام
residence permit		*public safety*	
shahāda al-ṣiḥḥa	شهادة الصحة	ta'mīn	تـأمين
health certificate		*insurance*	
wakīl	وكيـل	'aqd al 'amal	عقـد العمـل
agent		*employment contract*	
wakāla	وكالـة	mandūb	منـدوب
agency		*representative*	
kātlb al 'adl	كاتب العـدل	mudīr	مـديــر
Notary public		*director, manager*	

mudīfa مضيفة
air hostess
al kuṭūṭ al jawwiya الخطوط الجوية
airlines
sharika al-ṭayrān شركة الطيران
airways (company)
tauqī' توقيع
signature
katm ختم
seal
muqaddim al-ṭalab مقدم الطلب
applicant
muwāfaqa موافقة
approval
qubūl قبول
acceptance
rafḍ رفض
rejection
tauẓīf توظيف
appointment
muwaẓẓaf موظف
employee
ta'shīra al-dukūl تأشيرة دخول
entry visa
ta'shīra murūr تأشيرة مرور
transit visa

ta'shīra 'amal تأشيرة عمل
employment visa
sāria al maf'ūl ساري المفعول
valid
ṣalāḥiya al-ta'shīra
صلاحية التأشيرة
validity of visa
ṣāliḥ صالح
useful,valid
lāgia لاغية
cancelled
ḥasab حسب
according to
rusūm رسوم
fee,tax
rasmī رسمي
official
ta'līmāt تعليمات
instructions
ṭalab طلب
demand/claim
'inda al-ṭalab عند الطلب
on demand
maṭlūb مطلوب
wanted
i'lān إعلان
announcement

shāğir شاغر
vacancy

ism إسم
name

jinsiya جنسية
nationality

makān al milād مكان الميلاد
place of birth

jawāz al-safar جواز السفر
passport

raqm al jawāz رقم الجواز
passport number

makān al iṣdār مكان الاصدار
place of issue

tarīk̲ al iṣdār تاريخ الاصدار
date of issue

tārik̲ al intiha' تاريخ الانتهاء
date of expiry

'unwān عنوان
address

mu'ahhilāt مؤهلات
qualifications

isti'dād lil'amal استعداد للعمل
capacity to work

musta'idd مستعد
prepared

kātib كاتب
writer

maktab مكتب
office

tansīq تنسيق
arrangement

nā'ib نائب
deputy

shahāda شهادة
certificate

aṣl أصل
original

nusqa نسخة
copy

lifāfa لفافة
envelope

milaff ملف
file

k̲ibra خبرة
experience

mudda مدة
period

māni' مانع
objection

la māni' لا مانع
no objection

ḡarḍ غـرض
aim/objective

murāfiq مـرافق
companion/escort

mu'assasa مـؤسسـة
establishment

sharika شـركـة
business firm

ishtirāk إشتـراك
partnership/subscription

nashāṭ نشــاط
activity

nashīṭ نشـيط
energetic

taḡyīr تغيير
change/replacement

firqa فـرقـة
team/party

tafrīq تفـريـق
separation

bi mujib بمـوجب
in accordance with

ḡurfa al-tijāra غرفة التجـارة
chamber of commerce

taṣdīq تصـديـق
attestation

tajdīd تجديد
renewal

ittifāq إتـفــاق
agreement

بحثا علي السكن (فندق)

IN SEARCH OF ACCOMMODATION (HOTEL)

ṣabāḥ al k̲aiyr — صباح الخير
Good morning

ṣabāḥ al-nūr — صباح النور
Good morning (in reply)

ana qādim min New York — أنا قادم من نيو يورك
I am coming from New York

urīd g̅urfa — أريد غرفة
I want a room

al g̅urfa maḥjūza lak — الغرفة محجوزة لك
The room is reserved for you

hal turīd g̅urfa mufrada — هل تريد غرفة مفردة
Do you require a single room

aw muzawwada bi sarīrain — او مزودة بسريرين
Or (room) with two beds

hal fīha telephone — هل فيها تليفون
Is there telephone in it

kam yaum taskun — كم يوم تسكن
How many days will you stay

li usbū' faqaṭ — لاسبوع فقط
For a week only

kam ujrat al g̅urfa — كم اجرة الغرفة
How much is the room rent

k̲amsīn dollar yaumian خمسين دولور يوميا

$ 50 a day

tafaḍḍal ila al mudīr تفضل الي المدير

Please come to the manager

uktub al-tafāṣīl fi al-sijill اكتب التفاصيل في السجل

Write details in the register

utruk miftāḥ 'ind al k̲urūj اترك المفتاح عند الخروج

Leave the key while leaving

al miṣ'ad bi jānib al ḡurfa المصعد بجانب الغرفة

The lift is near the room

al maṭ'am fi al-daur al-t̲āni المطعم في الدور الثاني

The restaurant is on the 2nd floor.

al ḥallāq wa al ḡassāl a'iḍan الحلاق والغسال أيضا

Barber and washerman also

ḥauḍ al sibāḥa fī ḥadīqa al findaq حوض السباحة في حديقة الفندق

Swimming pool is in the garden of the hotel.

kam yaum taskun كم يوم تسكن

How many days do you stay.

li usbū' faqaṭ لاسبوع فقط

For a week only.

maktab al barīd qarīb min al findaq مكتب البريد قريب من الفندق

Post office is near the hotel.

lākin ayna al bank لكن أين البنك؟

But where is the bank?

'abr al-shāri' عبر الشارع

Across the road

AT THE RESTAURANT

Da'na nadhab ila al maṭ'am — دعنا نذهب الي المطعم

Let us go to the restaurant.

mā auqāt al faṭūr wa al ḡadā — ما اوقات الفطور والغداء

What are the timings for breakfast and lunch.

al faṭūr baina al ṯāmina wa al tāsia

الفطور بين الثامنة والتاسعة

Breakfast is between eight o'clock and nine

auqāt al 'ashā ḡair mu'ayyana — أوقات العشاء غير معينة

Supper timings are not fixed.

iḥḍar qāima al akl — احضر (جب) قائمة الاكل

Bring the menu (list)

ana 'atshān — أنا عطشان

I am thirsty

'aṣīr rummān min faḍlak — عصير رمان من فضلك

Pomegranate juice please.

ufaḍḍil qahwa — أفضل قهوة

I prefer coffee

bi al ḫalīb — بالحليب

With milk

ḵubz wa al-samak al-shawiy — الخبز والسمك الشوي

Bread and fish fry

mā' ma'dini — ماء معدني

Mineral water

urīd ḵubz wa jubn — أريد خبز وجبنة

I want bread and cheese

fāṭūra min faḍlak فاتورة من فضلك
Bill please
hal tadfa'a bi dollar هل تدفع بالدولور
Will you pay in dollar
urīd bait aw shaqqa أريد بيت أو شقة
I want a house or a flat
fi minṭaqa naẓīfa في منطقة نظيفة
In a clean locality
ufaḍḍil bait mafrūsh wa mukayyif أفضل بيتا مفروشا ومكيفا
I prefer a furnished and air conditioned house.
wa maṭbak̠ ma' furn و مطبخ مع فرن
And kitchen with oven
wa mā'ida wa karāsi wa kanba و مائدة وكراسي وكنبة
And a dining table, chairs and sofa.
naḥtāj ila k̠ādima lil-tanẓīf نحتاج الي خادمة للتنظيف
We require a maid servant for cleaning.
zaujatī taḥḍur al usbu'al qādim زوجتي تحضر الاسبوع القادم
ma' al atfāl مع الاطفال
My wife is coming next week with children.
aṭlub musā'ida fi shira' al āniya أطلب مساعدة في شراء الآنية
wa ba'ḍ al ḥājāt wa al kamāliyāt وبعض الحاجات والكماليات
I require help in purchasing utensils
and some necessities and luxury articles.

HOME بيـــت

kursī كرسي
chair
ṭāwala طاولـة
table
maq'ad مقعـد
seat
dulāb دولاب
cupboard
dulāb lil malābis دولاب للملابس
wardrobe
ḥadīqa حديقــة
garden
shajar شجـر
tree
nabāt نبـات
vegetation
zahra زهرة
flower
zīna زينـة
ornament
zukruf زخرف
decoration
bāb بـاب
door

qā'a قاعـة
hall
maṭbak مطبـخ
kitchen
kūb كـوب
cup
ibrīq ابريـق
kettle
mil'aqa ملعقـة
spoon
shauka شـوكـة
fork
ṣīnīya صينيـة
saucer,tray
ḥammām حمام
bath
istiḥmām استحمـام
bathing
mirḥāḍ مرحـاض
toilet
daura al miyāh دورة الميـاه
lavatory
daush دوش
shower

ḡurfa(t) al naum غرفة النوم
bedroom

ḡurfa(t) al julūs غرفة الجلوس
drawing room

ḥanafiya حنفيـة
tap

anābīb أنابيب
pipes

ṣabun صـابون
soap

fūṭa فـوطــة
towel

ḍau/noor ضـوء / نور
light

miṣbāḥ مصبـاح
lamp

furn فـرن
oven

saqf سقـف
roof/ceiling

sirdāb سـرداب
basement

taḥtu تحـت
beneath

fauqu فـوق
on top

nāfiḏa نـافذة
air hole

shubbāk شبـاك
window

shurfa شـرفــة
balcony

balāṭ بــلاط
tiled floor

'ataba عتبـة
threshhold

dih'līz دهليـز
corridor

saṭḥ سـطح
roof

jidār جـدار
wall

miḥrāb محـراب
prayer direction

ṯallāja ثلاجة
refrigerator

mi'ḏana مئـذنة
minaret

sullam سلـم
ladder

ḡurfa غـرفـة
room

liḥāf لحاف
quilt
sharshaf شرشف
bedsheet
masjid مسجد
mosque
kanīsa كنيسة
church
kanīs كنيس
synagogue
ma'bad معبد
temple
sajjāda سجادة
prayer rug,carpet

kahraba كهربة
electricity
miṣ'ad مصعد
lift
miftāh al kahraba مفتاح الكهربة
switch
ṣundūq صندوق
box
qufl قفل
lock
sarīr سرير
bed
maqadda مخدة
pill w
baṭṭaniya بطانية
blanket

مواد غذائية FOOD

dajāj دجاج
chicken

dajāj maqli دجاج مقلي
fried chicken

fark̲a فرخة
tender chicken

samak سمك
fish

shorba شوربة
soup

k̲all خل
vinegar

k̲ubz خبز
bread

zubda زبدة
butter

jubn جبن
cheese

murabba مربى
jam

ḥalwa حلوى
sweet item

baqlāwa بقلاوة
pastry

aruzz أرز
rice

qamḥ قمح
wheat

sha'īr شعير
barley

baiḍ بيض
egg

zait زيت
oil

dahn دهن
grease,fat,oil

samn سمن
cooking butter

biṭṭīk̲ بطيخ
melon

k̲aḍrawāt خضروات
vegetables

k̲ass خس
lettuce

fuṭūr فطور
breakfast

ḡadā غداء
lunch

'asha' عشاء
supper
wajba وجبة
meals
ḥalīb حليب
milk
laban لبن
sour milk
shāy شاي
tea
qahwa قهوة
coffee
'aṣīr fākiha عصير فاكهة
fruit juice
laḥm لحم
mutton
kabāb كباب
broiled meat
laḥm shawi لحم شوي
roasted meat
qashṭa قشطة
custard/cream
baskawīt بسكويت
biscuit
basbūsa بسبوسة
pastry

faṭīra فطيرة
cake
daqīq دقيق
flour
sukkar سكر
sugar
milḥ ملح
salt
'asal عسل
honey
filfil فلفل
pepper
bahārāt بهارات
spices
kusbara كسبرة
coriander
zamjabīl زنجبيل
ginger
qaranful قرنفل
clove
bāmiya باميا
ladies finger
laimūn ليمون
lemon
bāzinjān باذنجان
brinjal

baṭāṭis بطاطس
potatoes
kurunb كرنب
cabbage
qarnabīṭ قرنبيط
cauli flower
faṣūliya فصوليا
beans (European)
fūl mudammis فول مدمس
cooked beans
fūl sūdāni فول سوداني
peanuts
bunduq بندق
hazelnut
tuffāḥ تفاح
apple
k̲auk̲ خوخ
peach/plum
tīn تين
fig
lauz لوز
almonds
safarjal سفرجل
quince
k̲auf خوف
fear

muk̲īf مخيف
horrible
ḥubb حب
love/affection
maḥbūb محبوب
beloved
t̲um ثوم
garlic
sharāb شراب
fruit juice
fustaq فستق
pistachio
'adas عدس
lentils
baṣal بصل
onion
baqqāl بقال
grocer
salāṭa سلاطة
salad
ṭamāṭim طماطم
tomato
anānās اناناس
pineapple
burtuqāl برتقال
orange

bārid بارد
cold
mamlūḥ مملوح
saltish, saltine
muḥammaṣ محمص
roasted
maḥbūb محبوب
beloved
iḥsās احساس
feeling
k̲aṭar خطر
danger
k̲aṭīr خطير
serious
haḍama هضم
to digest
jambarī جمبري
shrimps
i'rbiyān إربيان
prawn
mu'tadil معتدل
proportionate
'ādi عادي
ordinary/common
k̲āṣ خاص
special

biṭṭīk̲ بطيخ
melon
balaḥ بلح
dates (raw)
tamr تمر
dates(dried)
jauz al hind جوز الهند
coconut
jauz جوز
walnut
mishmish مشمش
apricot
mauz موز
banana
māngou مانجو
mango
zaitūn زيتون
olive
ḥamiḍ حامض
sour
ḥulw حلو
sweet
murr مر
bitter
ḥārr حار
hot

حضــور فـي الشـركــة

REPORTING TO THE COMPANY

urīd muqābal(t) mudīr al-sharika   أريد مقابلة مدير الشركة

I wish to meet the manager of the company

tafaḍḍal huwa fī al-ġurfa   تفضل: هو في الغرفة

Please (come) he is in the room

ahlan wa sahlan   أهلا و سهلا

Welcome

ḥaḍartu min al hind   حضرت من الهند

I have come from India

'indī 'aqd al 'amal   عندي عقد العمل

I have with me employment contract.

haḏa ṣāliḥ li mudda sanatain   هذا صالح لمدة سنتين

This is valid for a period of two years.

al-tajdīd mumkin bimuwāfaqa al farīqain

التجديد ممكن بموافقة الفريقين

Renewal is possible with the consent of the two parties

sharṭan an takḍa'a iktibār 'amali   شرطا أن تخضع إختبار عملي

On the condition that it is subject to work test

wa ḏalika li ṯalāṯa ashhur   وذلك لثلاثة أشهر

(That is) for a period of 3 months

tastaḥiq ijāza sanawiya   تستحق إجازة سنوية

You are entitled to three months leave

al-rātib al-shahri ṯalāṯa alf riyāl saūdi

الراتب الشهري٣٠٠٠ ريال سعودي

The monthly salary is saudi riyals 3000/-

yalzam 'alaika an tahtam bi mawādd يلزم عليك أن تهتم بمـواد

al 'amal wa tanfid̲ awāmir al-sulṭa العمل وتنفيذ اوامر السلطة

You should be careful about the working hours and obey the orders of the authorities.

al kafil yaufuru lak al-sakan الكفيل يوفر لك السكن

wa suhūla al muwāṣalāt و سهولـة المـواصـلات

The sponsor shall provide you (with) accommodation and transport facilities.

'alaik an taḥtarim nizām al mamlaka عليك أن تحترم نظام المملكة

wa taqālid al balad وتقـاليـد البلـد

You should respect the laws of the Kingdom and convetions of the country.

lā budd min ijrā'āt al iqāma لابد من اجراءات الاقامـة

You should take care of residence permit proceedings.

id̲hab ila idāra(t) sijjil al ajānib اذهب الي ادارة سجل الاجانب

Go to the department of registration of foreigners

al 'amal fi al maṣna' muriḥ العمل في المصنع مريح

The work in the factory is comfortable

'adad al 'ummāl fīhi kat̲ir عـدد العمال فيه كثير

The number of workers (in it) are many

al mudir laṭif المـدير لطيف

The manager is a gentle person

auqāt dawām mu'ayyan اوقات الدوام معينـة

Working hours are specified

ana muhandis أنا مهنـدس

I am an engineer

'amlī murtaḅit bi al fannānīn عملي مرتبط بالفنـــانيـن

My work is connected with technicians

aqum bi wājibāti bi jidd wa ik̲lāṣ أقوم بواجباتي بجد واخـلاص

I do my duties with earnestness and sincerity

al-sharika t'anī bī الشركة تعني بي

The company takes care of me

wa tastak̲dim aṭibbā' muk̲taṣṣīn وتستخدم اطباء مختصين

It employs specialist doctors

makt̲tu sanatain fi al 'amal مكثت سنتين في العمل

I remained in the job for two years

ḥaṣaltu 'ala al ijāza li sharain حصلت علي الاجازة لمدة شهرين

I have obtained leave for a period of two months

wa saufa usāfir ba'du usbu' وسوف اسـافر بعد اسبـوع

I shall travel after two weeks

in shā'a Allah ان شـاء الله

God willing.

VOCABULARY

ta'dād تعـداد
counting

kaṯīr كثير
numerous

qalīl قليـل
few

istiḵdām استخـدام
employment

muḵtaṣṣ مـختـص
specialist

makaṯa مكث
remain/reside

huṣūl حصـول
obtaining

ḥaṣala حصل
to receive

suhūla سهولة
facility/convenience

lā budd لا بد
definitely

ḍarūri ضـروري
necessary

muwāṣala مواصلة
transportation

laṯīf لطيف
pleasant

waqt/auqāt وقت/أوقات
period of time

mu'ayyan معيـن
fixed

awqāt al-dawām أوقات الدوام
working hours

marbūṭ مربـوط
fastened/tied

murtabit مرتبط
linked

fannī فنـي
technician

fannān فنـان
artist/craftsman

jidd جـد
earnestness

iḵlāṣ إخـلاص
sincerity

wājib واجب
duty/assignment

'ināya عنايـة
care

taqālīd تقاليد
convention/tradition

ijra'āt qanūniya إجراءات قانونية
legal steps

iqāma إقامة
residence permit

maḥall al iqāma محل الاقامة
place of residence

idāra إدارة
administrative agency

idārī إداري
administrative

mudīr مدير
manager/director

ajnabi أجنبي
foreigner

murīḥ مريح
comfortable

ḥuḍūr حضور
presence

k̲aḍa'a خضع
to be subject to

tafaḍḍal تفضل
courteousness

ik̲tibār إختبار
test/experiment

ḥarām حرام
unlawful

iḥtirām إحترام
respect

rātibb راتب
salary

lāzim لازم
necessary

'inda al-ḍarūra عند الضرورة
in case of need

iltizām إلتزام
duty/commitment

ihtimām إهتمام
care/concern

muhim مهم
important

mādda/mawād مادة/مواد
material

mawād tijāriya مواد تجارية
trading commodities

mawād k̲ām مواد خام
raw material

niẓām نظام
regulations

tanẓīm تنظيم
control

sharṭ شرط
condition
taufīq توفيق
success
mufāraqa مفارقة
separation
ḥaqq حق
one's due
taḥqīq تحقيق
verification/realization
ijāza إجازة
permission
jā'iz جائز
lawful

tanfīd تنفيذ
carrying out
lajma tanfīdia لجنة تنفيذية
executive committee
'amr - a'wāmir أمر – أوامر
instruction/orders
sulṭa سلطة
authority
sakan سكن
dwelling/abode
sukūn سكون
tranquility
kafīl كفيل
guarantor/sponnsor
makfūl مكفول
person sponsored

الســــــوق
THE MARKET

adhab ila al-sūq al markazi — أذهب إلي السوق المركزي
I am going to the central market

hada sūq kabīr — هـذا سوق كبير
This is a big market

fīhi dakākīn katīra — فيـه دكاكيـن كثيرة
There are many shops in it

tābi'a lil jam'iya al-ta'āwuniya — تابعة للجمعية التعاونية
This is controlled by the Co-operative society

yubā' fīhi ḥajāt al-ṭabak — يبـاع فيه حاجات الطبخ
Cooking requirements are sold in it

hal al kaḍrawāt maujūda — هل الخضروات موجودة
Are vegetables available

na'am wa fawākih aiḍan — نعم وفـواكـه أيضا
Yes and fruits too

'aṭinī nisf kīlo baṭaṭis — أعطيني نصف كيلو بطاطس
Give me 1/2 kilo of potatoes

wa rub' kīlo tum wa basal — وربع كيلو ثوم و بصل
And 1/4 kilo of garlic and onion

hal yakfi — هل يكفـي
Is it sufficient

'atini kīlo laḥm — أعطيني كيلو لحم
Give me a kilo of meat

iqṭa' wa ḍa' fi al kīs — اقطع وضع في الكيس
Cut it (into pieces) and put it in the bag

kam al-ṯaman — كم الثمن

What is the price

ṯalāṯa riyāl lil kīlo — ثلاثة ريال للكيلو

Three Riyals a kilo

haḏa ḡāli jiddan — هذا غالي جدا

This is very expensive

bal raḵīṣ — بل رخيص

But it is cheap

la musāwama min faḍlak — لا مساومة من فضلك

No bargaining please

nasītu an ashtari al-samak — نسيت أن اشتري السمك

I have forgotten to purchase fish

haḏa fi janāḥ āḵar — هذا في جناح آخر

This is in another wing

al-sūq mamlū' bil zabā'in — السوق مملوء بالزبائن

The market is full of customers.

narj' ila al bait — نرجع إلي البيت

We shall return home

nashtarī dajāj wa al-samak ḡadan — نشتري دجاج وسمك غدا

We will purchase chicken and fish tomorrow

ana bi ḥāja ila lauz wa al-tamar — أنا بحاجة إلي اللوز والتمر

I need almond(s) and dates

aḏhab ila al baqqāl — أذهب إلي البقال

I will go to the grocer

'atinī kīlo mishmish wa fustaq — أعطيني كيلو مشمش وفستق

Give me a kilo of apricot and pistachio

VOCABULARY (GENERAL)

na'am نعم
yes, indeed

lā لا
not, no

aiḍan أيضا
also, too

'aṭiya عطية
gift

wafara وفر
to provide

wafratan وفرة
plenty

kafa كفى.
to be enough

kifāya كفاية
sufficient

qiṭ'a قطعة
piece

kīs كيس
bag, purse

waḍ' وضع
laying down

ḥāja حاجة
need

baqqāl بقال
grocer

taslīm تسليم
handing over

yā salām يا سلام
exclamation of amazement

maḵzan مخزن
store

maḥall محل
shop, locality

sūq سوق
market

dukkān دكان
shop

bai' بيع
sale

sharā' شراء
buy

kaṯīr كثير
plenty

qalīl قليل
little

jam'iya جمعية
association, society

jam'iya ta'āwuniya جمعية تعاونية
co-opperative society
tābi' تابع
dependent
mulḥaqa ملحقة
affiliated to
ṭabbāk̲ طباخ
cook
maujūd موجود
available, found
t̲aman ثمن
price
ḡāli غالي
costly
ḡalā غلاء
high prices

rak̲īṣ رخيص
cheap
jiddan جدا
very much
musāwama مساومة
bargaining
nasiya نسي
to forget
janāḥ جناح
wing, part of a building
āk̲ar آخر
another
zabūn زبون
customer
rujū' رجوع
return

شـــراء الأقـمشة

PURCHASING CLOTHES

nad̲hab ila sūq al aqmisha — نذهب إلي سوق الأقمشـة

Let us go to the textile market

urīd shirā qumāsh — أريـد شـراء قماش

I wish to purchase cloth

ayy nau' turīd — أي نوع تريـد

Which variety (of cloth) do you want

quṭn wa ṣūf — قطـن و صـوف

Cotton and woollen (material)

kam mitr — كم متـر

How many meters

'ashra amtār min nau' jayyid — عشرة أمتار من نوع جيد

Ten meters of excellent quality

hal turīd bi akmām ṭawīla am qaṣīra — هل تريد بأكمام طويلة أم قصيرة

Do you want it in long breadth or short breadth

bi akmām ṭawīla — بـأكمام طويلـة

In long breadth

id̲an had̲a ḡāli — إذا هذا غـالي

In that case it is costly

lā ba's — لا بــأس

Never mind (there is no objection to it)

hal ta'rifu k̲ayyāṭ mumtāz — هل تعرف خياط ممتاز

Do you know any good tailor

n'am hua bi jānib al-dukkān نعم هو بجانب الدكان

Yes he is near the shop

urīd tafṣīl qamīṣ wa badla أريد تفصيل قميص و بدلة

I wish to stitch a shirt and a suit

mata turīduhu متي تريده

When do you want it

al usbū' al qādim ألاسبوع القادم

The next week

ayy k̲idma uk̲ra أي خدمةأخري

Any other service

ayn maḥall al ḡasīl wa al kawi أين محل الغسيل والكواء

Where is the laundry

al ittijāh al āk̲ar ألاتجاه الآخر

In the other direction

TAILORING REQUIREMENTS

ṭawīl طويل
tall, high

ṭūl طول
length

qaṣīr قصير
short

qāṣir قاصر
minor

lā ba's لا بأس
never mind

k̲ayyāṭ خياط
tailor

mumtāz ممتاز
excellent

imtiyāz إمتياز
distinction

jānib جانب
portion, section

mak̲zan مخزن
shop, storage

ḡassāl غسال
washerman

ḡassāla غسالة
washing machine

muḡtasal مغتسل
washroom

'abara عبر
to cross

shāri' شارع
street

mashrū' مشروع
project

ishrāf إشراف
supervision

mushrif مشرف
superintendent

ittijāh إتجاه
direction

tujāh تجاه
in front of

yamīn يمين
right side

yasār يسار
left side

badla بدلة
suit

qumāsh قماش
cloth

qamīṣ قميص
shirt

tafṣīl تفصيل
cutting of cloth

min tafṣīl من تفصيل
tailored by

tafṣīlī تفصيلي
detailed

infiṣāl إنفصال
separation

mata متي
when?

qādim قادم
one arriving, next

taqdīm تقديم
offering

jihāz جهاز
equipment

nau' نوع
type, sort

quṭn قطن
raw cotton

ṣūf صوف
wool

mitr متر
meter

jayyid جيد
good

ajwad أجود
better

kamm كم
amount, quantity

jāhiz جاهز
ready

في مكتب البريد

AT THE POST OFFICE

ana amām maktab al barīd — أنا أمام مكتب البريد

I am in front of the post office

sa'ai al barīd yak̲ruj min al maktab — ساعي البريد يخرج من المكتب

Postman leaves the office

m'a hu ḥaqība — معه حقيبة

(He has) with him a bag

wa-fi-ha rasā'il min dāk̲il wa k̲ārij al bilād — وفيها رسائل من داخل وخارج البلاد

In it are letters from within and outside the country

aina shubbāk al-ṭawābi' — أين شباك الطوابع

Where is the stamp counter

urīd ṭawābi' barīdia — أريد طوابع بريدية

I want postal stamps

li irsāl al kitāb ila al k̲ārij — لارسال الخطاب إلي الخارج

to send the letter to foreign country

bi al barīd al jawwi — بالبريد الجوي

By airmail

idfa' k̲amsat riyāl — إدفع خمسة ريال

Pay SR 5/-

urīd irsāl haza al-ṭard — أريد إرسال هذا الطرد

I wish to send this parcel

min faḍlak imla isti'māra al g̅umruk — من فضلك إملاء استمارة الجمرك

Please fill up customs form

idhab ila al janāh al-ṭaliṭ إذهب إلي الجناح الثالث
Go to the third wing (counter)

hal ladaikum wasīla al barīd al-sari' هل لديكم وسيلة البريد السريع
Do you have speed post facility

'alaika an tadfa' akṯar عليك أن تدفع أكثر
You have to pay more

nafaqa ḡāliya نفقة غالية
Charges are costly

wa jihāz fāks وجهاز "فاكس"
And FAX apparatus (machine)

mā al-takālīf ما التكاليف
What are the charges

jihāz fāks mashḡūl al ān جهاز "فاكس مشغول الان
Fax machine is being used now

sajjil ismak wa intaẓir سجل إسمك وانتظر
Register your name and wait

irsal al barqiya awwal إرسل البرقية أولا
Send the telegram first

uqābil mudīr maktab al barīd أقابل مدير مكتب البريد

wa aṭlub ruḵṣa li fatḥ ṣundūq وأطلب رخصة لفتح صندوق

al barīd li isti'māli al ḵāṣṣ البريد لاستعمالي الخاص
I shall meet the chief of the post office
and apply for permission for opening a post box
for my personal use.

wāfaqa al mudīr وافق المدير
The chief agreed

wa i'ṭāni raqm ṣundūq al barīd وأعطاني رقم صندوق البريد
And gave me the post box number
urīd an atakallam bi al hātif al k̲āriji أريد أن أتكلم بالهاتف الخارجي
I wish to talk over the external phone
hād̲a mumkin هذا ممكن
This is possible
lākin fi auqāt mu'ayyana لاكن في أوقات معينة
But during specified hours
tafaḍḍal fi al-ṣabāḥ تفضل في الصباح
Please come in the morning
fi amān-i-allah في أمان الله
(Leave) In the protection of God
ma'a al-salāma مع السلامة
In the protection of God

PARTS OF THE BODY أجزاء الجسم

'ain عين
eye

muqla مقلة
eye-ball

k̲add خد
cheek

anf أنف
nose

ud̲un أذن
ear

fam فم
mouth

safa شفة
lip

sinn سن
tooth

nīra نيرة
gums (of the teeth)

ḍirs ضرس
wisdom tooth

qalb قلب
heart

ṣadr صدر
breast

baṭn بطن
stomach

ẓahr ظهر
back

fak̲d̲ فخذ
thigh

rukba ركبة
knee

sāq ساق
leg / thigh

ka'b كعب
ankle

rijl رجل
leg

qadam قدم
foot

jild جلد
skin

kibda كبدة
liver

jism جسم
body

ra's رأس
head

mukk مخ
brain

sha'r شعر
hair

jabha جبهة
forehead

jabin جبين
frontface

daqan ذخن
chin

wajh وجه
face

hajib حاجب
eyebrow

jafn جفن
eyelid

lu'ab لعاب
saliva

hanjara حنجرة
gullet

halq حلق
throat

raqaba رقبة
neck

kataf كتف
shoulder

ibt إبط
armpit

dira' ذراع
arm

yad يد
hand

kaffa كفة
palm

shahma شحمة
fat

'adalat عضلات
muscles

'asab أعصاب
nerves

shiryan شريان
artery

tihal طحال
spleen

am'a امعاء
intestines

ri'a رئة
lung

isb'a إصبع
finger

dil'a ضلع
rib

أسـرة FAMILY

ḥayāh حياة
life
mīlād ميـلاد
birth
shahādat mīlād شهادة ميلاد
birth certificate
ṭufūla طفولـة
childhood
shāb شاب
young man
shabāb شـباب
youth
rajul رجل
man
rujūla رجولة
manhood
shaik̲ شيخ
elderly person
shaik̲uk̲a شيخوخة
old age
usra أسرة
family
ab أب
father
umm أم
mother
uk̲t أخت
sister
imra'a إمرأة
woman
k̲utūba خطوبة
betrothal
'arūsa عروسة
bride
'arīs عريس
bridegroom
zauj زوج
husband, one of a pair
zauja زوجة
wife
'amm عـم
uncle
k̲āla خـالـة
aunt
jadd جـد
grand father
ḥafīd حفيد
grandson

مشــاورة مــع الـطـبيب
CONSULTING THE DOCTOR

urīd al-ḏihāb ila al-ṭabīb — أريد الذهاب إلي الطبيب

I wish to go to the (physician)

al mustashfa al 'ām qarīb min al manzil

المستشفي العام قريب من المنزل

The General Hospital is near the residence

'iyāda doctor Aḥmad ba'īd — عيـادة دكتور أحمد بعيد

The clinic of Dr. Ahmad is far away

ṣabāḥ al ḵair — صباح الخيـر

Good morning

kaifa ḥāluka — كيف حالك

How are you

ash'ur bi alam fi al baṭn — أشعر بالم في البطن

I feel pain in the stomach

ra'si yulimni — رأسي يؤلمني

My head aches

indī qa'ai — عندي قيئ

I vomit

ash'ur bi ḍu'f fi al jism — أشعر بالضعف في الجسـم

I feel physically weak

hal 'indaka shahiya lil akl — هل عندك شهية للاكل

Have you appetite (for food)

arini lisanak — أريني لسانك

Show me your tongue

hal tash'ur bi marāra fi al fam هل تشعر بمرارة في الفم

Do you feel bitterness in the mouth

ik̲la al kamīs إخلع القميص

Remove the shirt

istariḥ huna إستريح هنا

Relax / lie down here

tanaffas bi 'amq تنفس بعمق

Take a deep breath

sauqīs darjat al ḥarāra سأقيس درجة الحرارة

I shall take (measure) the temperature

ifḥas ḍag̲t al-dam أفحص ضغط الدم

Examine blood pressure

irsal 'ayyina min al baul ila al muk̲tabar

إرسل عينية من البول إلي المختبر

Send urine sample to the laboratory

taḥlīl al-dam wa al birāz ḍarūri تحليل الدم والبراز ضروري

Analysis of blood and feces is necessary.

lā dā'i lil k̲auf لا داعي للخوف

There is no need to fear

al maraḍ basīṭ المرض بسيط

The disease is simple

ist'amal had̲ihi al 'aqaqīr أستعمل هذه العقاقير

Use this medicine (tablets)

taḥtāj ḥuqna تحتاج حقنة

You require injection

id̲hab ila al muk̲tabar إذهب ألي المختبر

Go to the laboratory

ishtari dawā min al-ṣaidalia أشتري دواء من الصيدلية

Purchase medicine from the pharmacy

la tatruk al-dawā li yowmain لا تترك الدواء ليومين

Do not leave the medicine for two days

kud rāha li usbū' خذ راحة لاسبوع

Take rest for a week

irja' ilayya id 'ādat al 'illa إرجع إليّ إذ عادت العلة

Come again to me if the ailment returns (repeats)

atamanna lak al-ṣiḥḥa wa al 'āfiya أتمنى لك الصحة والعافية

Wish you fine health

ashkuruka yā doctor أشكرك يا دكتور

I thank you Doctor

COMMON DISEASES

nauba qalbiya نوبة قلبية
heart attack

saratān سرطان
cancer

su'āl سعال
cough

imsāk إمساك
constipation

qabḍ قبض
constipation

ishāl إسهال
diarrhea

taḥlīl تحليل
analysis

bawāsīr بواسير
piles

ḍagt al-dam ضغط الدم
blood preassure

hubūṭ هبوط
feebleness

zukām زكام
cold

ḥumma حمى
fever

tyfoid تائفويد
typhoid

malariya ملاريا
malariya

ṭa'ūn طاعون
plague

wabā' وباء
epidemic

ḍarbat al-shams ضربة الشمس
sunstroke

nabḍ نبض
pulse

maraḍ مرض
ailment, disease

marīḍ مريض
sick person

amrāḍ mu'diya أمراض معدية
contagious diseases

a'ma عمي
blind

aṣamm, ṣumm أصم / صم
deaf

abkam أبكم/بكم
dumb

aḵras *mute*	أخرس	yarqān *jaundice*	يرقان
muṣādama *collision*	مصادمة	'aṣabi *nervous*	عصبي
ṣadma *shock / stroke*	صدمة	naḥīl *slim*	نحيل
ḥādiṯ *accident , mishap*	حادث	samīn *stout*	سمين
ḍa'īf *weak*	ضعيف	qarḥa *ulcer*	قرحة
ḍu'f *weakness*	ضعف	tasammum *poisoning*	تسمم
qawiy *strong*	قوي	jurḥ *wound / injury*	جرح
quwa *strength*	قوة	alam *pain*	ألم
ta'ab *exertion / toil*	تعب	mu'lim *painful*	مؤلم
ta'bān *exhausted*	تعبان	ḥurqa *burning sensation*	حرقة
sall *tuberculosis*	سل	dummal *abscess / tumor*	دمل
fālij *paralysis*	فالج	jarrāḥ *surgeon*	جرّاح
judari *smallpox*	جدري	ṭabīb *physician*	طبيب

ṭabīb asnān طبيبأسنان
dentist

ashi'a أشعة
x-ray

maraḍ al-sukkari مرض السكري
diabetes

naẓīf نظيف
clean

wasik̲ وسخ
dirty

nafas نفس
breath

tanaffus تنفس
respiration

dam دم
blood

ṭūl / ṭawīl طول / طويل
height / tall

'arḍ / 'arīḍ عرض / عريض
width / wide

wazn وزن
weight

t̲aqīl ثقيل
heavy / cumbersome

sam' / sami' سمع / سميع
hearing ,listener

baṣar بصر
eye sight

baraṣ برص
leprosy

junūn جنون
lunacy

naum نوم
sleep

araq أرق
sleeplessness, insomnia

rumātism روماتزم
rhematism

anf al ḥassāsa أنف الحساسة
scanning

TRANSPORT AND EQUIPMENTS

helikopter هليكوبـــــتر
helicopter
mizān ميزان
balance
hātif هاتف
telephone / call
tilifūn تلفون
telephone
tilivisyon تلفزيون
television
musạwwira مصورة
camera
būq بوق
horn / trumpet
midyā' مـذياع
radio set
rādiyo راديو
radio
idā'a إذاعـة
announcement
idā'a al akbār إذاعة الاخبار
newscast
sayyāra سيـارة
car / automobile

sāiq سائق
driver
qiyāda قيادة
driving
ruksa qiyāda رخصة قيادة
driving permit
mauqif bus موقف بس
bus stop
wuqūf وقوف
stop / halt
katar خطـر
danger
al-najda النجدة
help! help!
shurṭa شـرطة
police
dār al-shurṭa دار الشرطة
police station
midfa' مدفع
gun / cannon
darrāja دراجة
bicycle
'araba عربة
coach

sayyāra سيارة
car / automobile

qiṭār قطار
train

shāḥina شاحنة
lorry

markab مركب
ship

safīna سفينة
boat

bāḵira باخرة
steamer

ḡawwāsa غوّاصة
submarine

zauraq زورق
steam launch

dabbāba دبابة
tank

ṭā'ira طائرة
airplane

rādār رادار
radar

mirwaha مروحة
fan

miḵraṭa مخرطة
lathe

ālat al ḵiyāṭa آلة الخياطة
sewing machine

mūs موس
razor

miqaṣṣ مقص
scissors

dabbāba دبابة
tank

sā'a ساعة
clock

sā'at yad ساعة يد
wrist watch

sā'at munabbiha ساعة منبهة
alarm clock

miqyās مقياس
measuring instrument

al miqyās al kahrabāi
electrometer المقياس الكهربائي

kawa كوى
to press, iron, laundry

miknasa مكنسة
sweeper

sikkīn سكين
knife

shauka شوكة
fork

k̲anjar خنجر
dagger

fa's فأس
axe

ibra إبرة
needle

dabbūs دبوس
safety pin

qaus قوس
bow

sahm سهم
arrow

saif سيف
sword

musaddas مسدس
revolver

banduqiya بندقية
rifle

ENVIRONMENT

ḏahab ذهب
gold

fiḍḍa فضة
silver

marjān مرجان
small pearls

lu'lu' لؤلؤ
pearls

nafṭ نفط
petroleum

marj مرج
meadow

ḡāba غابة
forest

wādi واد
valley

ṭabī'a طبيعة
nature

falak فلك
planets

majarra مجرة
galaxy

shams شمس
sun

qamar قمر
moon

kasf كسف
eclipse

ma'din معدن
metal, mine

ḥadīd حديد
iron

nuḥās نحاس
copper

raṣāṣ رصاص
lead

ismant اسمنت
cement

rayyiḥ ريح
windy

kaun كون
universe

kaun كون
existence

'ālam عالم
world / cosmos

mā' ماء
water

arḍ أرض
earth

hawā' هواء
air / atmosphere

nār/ḥariqa نار/حريقة
fire

ḥarrāqa حراقة
torpedo

zalāzil زلازل
earthquake

shallāl شلال
waterfall

ḥauḍ حوض
tank / pool

baḥr بحر
sea

muḥīt محيط
ocean

qanāh قناة
canal

ḵalīj خليج
gulf

bi'r بئر
well / spring

nahr نهر
river

fayḍān فيضان
flood

sail سيل
flood (torrential stream)

burkān بركان
volcano

maṭar مطر
rain

barq برق
lightning

'āṣifa عاصفة
storm

samā' سماء
sky

kaukab كوكب
star

najm نجم
star

shajar شجر
tree

jabal جبل
mountain

nabāt نبات
plants

لـدي الـبـنـك

AT THE BANK

assalāmu 'alaikum — الـسـلام عليـكـم
Greetings (peace be on you)

wa 'alaikum as-salām — وعليكـم الـســلام
Reply to the traditional greetings

urīd aftaḥ ḥisāb — أريد افتـح حسـاب
I want to open an account

ana min ḵārijal balad — أنـا مـن خـارج البلـد
I am a foreigner

mā hia al-mustanadat al-maṭlūba — مـا هي المستنـدات المطلوبـة؟
What are the documents required?

mai al awrāq al lāzima — مـعي الاوراق اللازمـة
I have with me the necessary papers.

'aṭinī daftar shekāt — أعطينـي دفتـر شكات
Please give me the cheque book

urīd saḥb mablāgh — أريـد سحـب مبلـغ
I wish to draw an amount

mata uftaḥ al-bank? — متي يفتـح البـنـك؟
When does the bank open?

fi al-saa at-ṯāmina ṣabāḥan — في الســاعـة الثـامنـة صبـاحـا
At 8 o'clock in the morning

uḡlaq at-ṯaniya ẓuhran — يغلق الســاعة الثـانيـة ظهـرا
It closes at 2 o'clock in the afternoon.

ugabil mudīr al ḥisābāt — اقابل مدير الحسابات

I will meet the accounts manager.

aṭlub minhu kashf al-ḥisāb — اطلب منه كشف الحساب

I will demand from him a statement of account.

lā 'arif ma tabqa min al mablaḡ — لا أعرف ما تبقى من المبلغ

I do not know what is the balance

ma hua la-niẓām li taḥwīl al mablaḡ — ما هو النظام لتحويل المبلغ

What is the procedure for transfering money

id̲n min al bank ḍarūri — إذن من البنك ضروري

Permission from the bank is necessary

hal li an adf'a d̲arāib — هل لي أن أدفع ضرائب

Have I to pay taxes

intaẓar ḥatta ushāwir al mudīr — إنتظر حتى أشاور المدير

Wait till I consult the Director

ayy k̲idma uk̲ra — أي خدمة أخرى

Any other service

shukran li ta'āwunikum — شكرا لتعاونكم

Thanks for your cooperation

VOCABULARY

BANKING AND CORRESPONDENCE

k̲āriji خارجي
external

dak̲ilī داخلي
internal

sanad سند
support

mustanadāt مستندات
documents

maṭlūb مطلوب
wanted/due

muṭalaba مطالبة
demand/call

waraq ورق
paper

lāzim لازم
necessary

ḥisāb حساب
account

muḥāsib محاسب
accountant

saḥb سحب
withdrawal

mablaḡ مبلغ
amount

mata متى
when

kashf كشف
list/schedule

niẓām نظام
law/system

ayy أي
any/which/what?

umla عملة
money

baqiyya بقية
residue

niẓām نظام
law/system

taḥwīl تحويل
transfer

biṭaqat itimād بطاقة اعتماد
credit card

shēk شيك
cheque

id̲n إذن
permission

'aun عون
help/aid

ta'āwun تعاون
cooperation

āk̲ar آخر
another/one more

marra uk̲ra مرة اخرى
once more

ayy أي
any/which/what

ayyuma أيما
whatever

'umla ṣa'ba عملة صعبة
hard currency

'umla عملة
currency

fath ḥisāb فتح حساب
opening an account

ḍarūri ضروري
necessary

ḍarūra ضرورة
necessity

daf' دفع
pay/push

ḍarība ضريبة
tax

intiẓar انتظار
waiting/expecting

mushāwara مشاورة
consultation

mustashār مستشار
consultant

k̲idma خدمة
service/work

fatūra فاتورة
bill

زيـارة صـديـق
VISITING A FRIEND

ṣabāḥ al k̲air ya k̲ālid	صباح الخير يا خالد
Good morning Khalid	
ṣabāḥ al-nur ya nafīs	صباح النور يا نفيس
Good morning Nafis	
tafaḍḍal ijlis	تفضل إجلس
Please come and sit	
kaifa al-ṣiḥḥa	كيف الصحة
How is the health	
ataqid 'ala ma urām	أعتقد علي ما يرام
I believe it is as expected	
al ḥamdu li-llāhi 'ala kulli ḥāl	الحمد لله علي كل حال
Praise be to God in all conditions	
ana sa'īd bi ziyāratika	أنا سعيد بزيارتك
I am happy with your visit	
kaifa al ahl	كيف الأهل
How is the family	
hal tasmaḥ lī 'an a'takallam bi al-tilifun	هل تسمح لي أن أتكلم بالتلفون
Will you permit me to talk over the phone	
bikull surūr	بكل سرور
With great pleasure	
tafaḍḍal al ḡada' jāhiz	تفضل الغداء جاهز
Please come, the lunch is ready	

lastu bi jau'ān	لست بجوعـان
I am not hungry	
ma'd̲ira yā saidi	معذرة يا سيدي
Excuse me sir	
ana aṭshān, mā' min faḍḍlak	أنا عطشان ماء من فضلك
I am thirsty, water please	
huwa a'k̲ī	هو أخي
He is my brother	
ana sa'īd bi ma'rifatihi	أنا سعيد بمعرفته
I am happy to know him	
ḥāna al waqt lil ḡadā	حان الوقت للغداء
Lunch time has come	
nastamir bi al ḥadīt̲ ba'du	نستمر بالحديث بعد
Let us continue the conversation later	
al-ṭa'ām lad̲īd̲	الطعام لذيذ
The food is tasty	
al laḥm wa al k̲aḍrawāt wa al fawākih	اللحم والخضروات والفواكه
Meat, vegetables and fruits	
shukran 'ala ḥusn al-ḍiyāfa	شكرا علي حسن الضيافة
Thanks for fine hospitality	
mamnunin giddan	ممنونين جدا
(We are) much obliged	

VOCABULARY (GENERAL)

ḍiyāfa ضيافة
hospitality

muḍīf مضيف
host

muḍīfa مضيفة
hostess

shākir شاكر
thankful

mamnūn ممنون
obliged

samaḥa سمح
permit

masmūḥ مسموح
permitted

surūr سرور
joy

jāhiz جاهز
ready

ma'ḏira معذرة
begging excuse

ba'du بعد
afterwards

ṭa'ām طعام
food

ṣadīq صديق
friend

ahl أهل
relatives

jau'ān جوعان
hungry

'aṭshān عطشان
thirsty

'aduw عدو
enemy

huwa هو
he

huwiya هوية
identity

sa'īd سعيد
happy

ḥazīn حزين
sad

ma'rifa معرفة
acquaintance / knowledge

ḥīnama حينما
while

istimrār إستمرار
continuation

ḥadīt حديث
talk

ḥādiṯa حادثة
accident

laḏīḏ لذيذ
delicious

ziyāra زيارة
visit

zāir زائر
visitor

ṣadīq صديق
friend

ḵair خير
best

nūr نور
light

ṣiḥḥa صحة
health

kull كل
entire / all

ḥāl حال
condition

ḥaul حول
power

quwwa قوة
power

الحيوانات والطيور
ANIMALS AND BIRDS

baṭṭ بط
duck
ḥamām حمام
dove
bulbul بلبل
nightingale
hudhud هدهد
hoopoe
na'ām نعام
ostrich
būm بوم
owl
ḡurāb غراب
crow
sulḥafāh سلحفاة
tortoise
samak سمك
fish
shabbūṭ شبوط
fish from Euphrates
dulfīn دلفين
dolphin
sārdīn ساردين
sardines

nāmūsa ناموسة
mosquito
ba'ūḍ بعوض
mosquitoes
fār فار
rat
naml نمل
ant
farāsha فراشة
butterfly
ḥashara حشرة
insect
ḏubāb ذباب
fly
nasr نسر
vulture
naḥl نحل
bee
babḡā' ببغاء
parrot
dīk ديك
cock
dajāj دجاج
hen

timsāḥ تمساح
crocodile

ṯa'lab ثعلب
fox

jamūs جاموس
buffalo

ḥimār حمار
donkey

ḥayya - ṯubān حية / ثعبان
snake

dubb دب
bear

ḏi'b ذئب
wolf

zarāfa زرافة
giraffe

ḵinzīr خنزير
pig

shāh(t) شاة
sheep / ewe

ḵarūf خروف
lamb / sheep

qiṭ قط
cat

quṭaiṭa قطيطة
kitten

ḡanam غنم
small cattle

bahīma بهيمة
cattle

ṭaūs طاؤوس
peacock

fahd فهد
panther

fīl فيل
elephant

namir نمر
tiger

kalb كلب
dog

qird قرد
monkey

ḡurilla غوريلا
gorilla

asad أسد
lion

jamal / ibil جمل / إبل
camels

arnab أرنب
rabbit

baqara بقرة
cow

'ankabūt عنكبوت
spider

barḡūt برغوث
shimps

'aqrab عقرب
scorpion

shahīn شاهين
Indian falcon

bāż باز
falcon

ṣaqr صقر
hawk

jarād جراد
locust

عيـــــد سعيـــــد

THE AUSPICIOUS 'ID

al yaum 'id al fiṭr al mubārak — أليوم عيد الفطر المبارك

Today is the auspicious "'Id al Fitr.

wa 'uṭla bi munāsiba al 'īd — وعطلة بمناسبة العيد

And it is a holiday on account of the festival

naḏhab li ziyāra ṣadīquna Mohammad — نذهب لزيارة صديقنا محمد

We shall visit our friend Mohammad

huwa walad mu'addab — هو ولد مؤدب

He is a well mannered boy

ak̲ūhu fī al-ṯānawia — أخوه في الثانوية

His brother is in the secondary school

ahlan wa sahlan wa marḥaban — أهلا وسهلا ومرحبا

Welcome to you, You are most welcome

'īdukum mubārak — عيدكم مبارك

May the festival be auspicious

kull 'ām wa antum bi k̲air — كل عام وأنتم بخير

May you be in prosperity every year

a'addat al usra a'nwā' min al-ṭa'ām — أعدت الاسرة أنواع من الطعام

The family has prepared a variety of dishes

wa qaddamū al halwa wa al bārid awallan

وقدموا الحلوي والبارد أوّلاً

They offered sweets and cool drinks first

fariḥu bi ziāratrina — فرحوا بزيارتنا

They were happy with our visit

al-ṣiḡār mashḡūlin bi la'bal computer

الصغار مشغولين بلعب الكمبوتر

The younger ones were busy with computer games

wa al kibār yatakallamūn والكبار يتكلمون

The elders are conversing

haḏa yaum al farḥ wa al-sa'āda هذا يوم الفرح والسعادة

This is a day of joy and happiness

nanfuq 'ala al fuqarā ننفق علي الفقراء

We spend (charities) on the poor

wa nashkur Allah 'ala ni'amhi ونشكر الله علي نعمه

And thank God for His bounties

ittafaqna 'ala al-nuzha اتفقنا علي النزهة

We agreed to go on an excursion

wa aḵtarnā minṭaqa siyyāḥia واخترنا منطقة سياحية

And we chose a tourist place

iḏan nasta'idd إذا نستعد

In that case we have to prepare

wa nuḡādir ḡadan ṣabāḥan ونغادر غدا صباحا

We leave tomorrow morning

nuzha li yaum kāmil نزهة ليوم كامل

Recreation for a complete day

furṣa ṣa'īda فرصة سعيدة

A happy occasion

VOCABULARY (GENERAL)

'īd عيد
festival
'īd al fiṭr عيد الفطر
festival breaking Ramdan fast
'īd al aḍḥā عيد الأضحى
festival of 10th zu'lhijja
'īd mīlād عيد ميلاد
christmas
sana mīlādia سنة ميلادية
year of Christian era
maulid an-nabiy مولد النبي
Prophet's birthday
sa'āda سعادة
bliss, prosperity
baraka بركة
blessing
mubārak مبارك
lucky
'uṭla عطلة
holiday
mu'addib مؤدب
well-mannered
'adda عد
arrange

musta'id مستعد
prepared
ṣağīr صغير
small / young
kabīr كبير
big / large
farḥa فرحة
joy
farḥān فرحان
cheerful
faqīr فقير
poor man
ğaniy غني
wealthy
minṭaqa منطقة
area / zone
sawwāḥ سواح
tourist
riḥla رحلة
travel / journey
usra أسرة
family

TIME, DAYS AND MONTHS

sā'a ساعة
time
daqīqa دقيقة
minute
ṯāniya ثانية
second (time unit)
yaum يوم
day
usbū' أسبوع
week
shahr شهر
month
ṣabāh صباح
morning
nahăr نهار
day time
ḍuḥā ضحى
forenoon
ẓuhr ظهر
midday (afternoon)
masā' مساء
evening
lail ليل
night

qabl al-ẓuhr قبل الظهر
in the forenoon
b'ad al-ẓuhr بعد الظهر
in the afternoon
marra مرة
once
marratain مرتين
twice
marrăt مرات
several times
sana سنة
year
ṣaif صيف
summer
rabī' ربيع
spring
ḵarīf خريف
autumn
shitā' شتاء
winter

sana masihiya سنة مسيحية

Months of Christian Era

kānūn al-ṯāni كانون ثاني/يناير

January (Yanair)

shubāṭ/Fabrayir شباط / فبراير

February

āḏār/mars آذار / مارس

March

nīsān/ibril نيسان/إبريل

April

ayyār/mayu ايار/مايو

May

ḥazīrān/yuniyo حزيران/يونيو

June

tammūz/yuliya تموز/يوليو

July

ăb/agustus آب/أغسطس

August

ailūl/sibtambar أيلول/سبتمبر

September

tishrīn al awwal تشرين الاول

October أكتوبر

tishrīn al-ṯāni تشرين الثاني

November نوفمبر

kānūn al awwal كانون الاول

December ديسمبر

Sana Hijriya سنة هجرية

Months of Muslim Era

muharram محرم

First Islamic month

safar صفر

name of second month

rabi' al awwal ربيع الأول

3rd month

rabi' al-tani ربيع الثاني

4th month

jumadi al ula جمادي الاولي

5th month

jumadi al akira جمادي الآخرة

6th month

rajab رجب

7th month

sha'ban شعبان

8th month

ramadan رمضان

9th month

shawwal شوال

10th month

dul qa'da ذو القعدة

11th month

dul hijja ذو الحجة

12th month

WEEK DAYS

Sunday	yaum al a'ḥad	يوم الأحد
Monday	yaum al iṯnain	يوم الاثنين
Tuesday	yaum al-ṯulāṯā	يوم الثلاثاء
Wednesday	yaum al arba'ā	يوم الأربعاء
Thursday	yaum al ḵamīs	يوم الخميس
Friday	yaum al jum'a	يوم الجمعة
Saturday	yaum al-sabt	يوم السبت

NUMBERS	الاعداد
wāḥid	واحد
one	١
iṯnān	إثنان
two	٢
ṯalāṯa	ثلاثة
three	٣
arba'a	أربعة
four	٤
ḵamsa	خمسة
five	٥
sitta	ستة
six	٦
sab'a	سبعة
seven	٧
ṯamāniya	ثمانية
eight	٨
tis'a	تسعة
nine	٩
'ashara	عشرة
ten	١٠

ṣifr	صفر
zero	٠
a'ḥada 'ashara	احد عشر
eleven	١١
iṯnā 'ashara	إثنا عشر
twelve	١٢
ṯalāṯa 'ashara	ثلاثة عشر
thirteen	١٣
arba't 'ashara	أربعة عشر
fourteen	١٤
ḵamsat 'ashara	خمسة عشر
fifteen	١٥
sittat 'ashara	ستة عشر
sixteen	١٦
sab'at 'ashara	سبعة عشر
seventeen	١٧
ṯamāniyat 'ashara	ثمانية عشر
eighteen	١٨
tis'at'ashara	تسعة عشر
nineteen	١٩
'ishrūn	عشرون
twenty	٢٠

'ashara	عشرة
ten	١٠
'ishrūn	عشرون
twenty	٢٠
t̲alat̲ūn	ثلاثون
thirty	٣٠
arba'ūn	أربعون
forty	٤٠
k̲amsūn	خمسون
fifty	٥٠
sittūn	ستون
sixty	٦٠
sab'ūn	سبعون
seventy	٧٠
t̲amanūn	ثمانون
eighty	٨٠
tis'ūn	تسعون
ninety	٩٠
mi'a	مائة
hundred	١٠٠

mi'a wa wāḥid	مائة وواحد
hundred and one	١٠١
mi'a wa tis'ūn	مائة وتسعون
hundred and ninety	١٩٠
mi'atān	مئتان
two hundred	٢٠٠
t̲alāt̲u mi'a	ثلاث مئة
three hundred	٣٠٠
arba'a mi'a	أربع مئة
four hundred	٤٠٠
k̲amsa imi'a	خمس مئة
five hundred	٥٠٠
sitta mi'a	ست مئة
six hundred	٦٠٠
sab'a mi'a	سبع مئة
seven hundred	٧٠٠
t̲amaniya mi'a	ثماني مئة
eight hundred	٨٠٠
tis'a mi'a	تسع مئة
nine hundred	٩٠٠
alf	ألف
thousand	١٠٠٠

alfān	ألفان	*two thousand*	٢٠٠٠
niṣf	نِصْفٌ	*half*	١/٢
tuluṯh	ثلث	*one third*	١/٣
rub'	ربع	*quarter*	١/٤
khamsoon fil mi'a	٥٠٪ خمسون في المائة		50%

Arabic is written from the right to the left, but Arabic numerals are written and read as in English from the left to the right. e-g: ١٩٩٦ (1996). In manuscripts number ٢ is usually written as (٢). The zero is indicated by a point (٠).

إعـــلانــات عـــامـــة

PUBLIC NOTICES

taḥḏir تحذير
warning

iḥḏar al kalb إحذر الكلب
beware of dogs

k̲aṭir خطر
dangerous

mamu' al lams ممنوع اللمس
don't touch

qif قف
stop

duk̲ūl دخول
entry

mamnū' al-duk̲ūl ممنوع الدخول
no admission

k̲urūj خروج
exit

lil ījār للايجار
for rent

al-ṭarīq masdud الطريق مسدود
road closed

maftūḥ مفتوح
opened

muqfal مقفل
locked

isti'lāmāt إستعلامات
information office

maḥjūz محجوز
reserved

daura al miyāh دورة المياه
latrine / toilet

laff yamīn لف يمين
turn right

laff yasār لف يسار
turn left

biṭāqat itimād بطـاقة اعتمـاد
credit card

daftar ḥisāb دفتر حساب
account register

shēk شيـك
cheque

mamnū'al-tadk̲īn ممنوع التدخين
smoking is prohibited

A NOTE ON ARABIC GRAMMAR

The basic principles which govern Arabic sentence structure are different from those of other languages. A sound knowledge of Arabic grammar is essential for a correct reading and understanding of an Arabic text, detailed explanation of the subject is beyond the scope of this book. A rudimentary knowledge of Arabic grammar is provided here with examples from the material that is available in the text itself.

VOWELS: Short vowels in Arabic - called 'haraka', *movement* - are indicated by signs in the form of strokes on or below the letter e.g : for "a" ---َ for "i" and "e" ---ِ for "u" and "o" ---ُ . Normally short vowels are not printed in a book or marked in the manuscripts except to ensure correct reading of the text.

Long vowels are indicated by three letters, الف for ā , و for ū and ō and ي for ī and ē .

DEFINITE ARTICLE: Arabic nouns or adjectives in the indefinite form are pronounced with "nunation" i.e: terminating in "n" sound. This sound is indicated by double vowel at the end of the word ---ً ---ٍ ---ٌ . The need for "nunation" does not arise when nouns and adjectives are definite. The definite article in Arabic is indicated by prefixing "al" ال to a word, e.g: كتاب kitabun *" a book"* will be pronounced as al kitab *" the book"*. But when "al" is prefixed to the words starting with letters in the category of "Sun letters".

ت ث د ذ ر ز س ش ص ض ط ظ ل ن

"l" remains silent and the first letter of the word that follows "ال" is pronounced twice, e.g: الشمس as-shamsu *"the sun"*. In such cases the method followed in this book in transliteration is to write "al" ال separately and connect it to the following word with a dash (-) al-shams *(the sun)*. الموظّف al muwazzaf "the officer", page No 6

The sign ــّـ shadda is used in Arabic to indicate a consonant occuring twice, one after the other, e.g. ربّ rabb *"lord"*

ABSENCE OF VOWEL: If a consonant is without a vowel its sound is assimilated with the following consonant, the sign used for this is ــْـ a small circle over the letter. e.g: مَنْظر manzar *"sight"* Here the first letter م (m) has a vowel, whereas the following letter ن (n) is without a vowel. Hence م and ن are assimilated and form a syllable. Refer to the words مفتوح and مغلق on page 3.

GENDER AND NUMBER: Nouns are divided into the masculine gender مذكر and the feminine gender مؤنث . A peculiar feature of the Arabic language is that its nouns, adjectives and verbs are divided into three numbers, Singular, Dual and Plural. In any sentence verbs and adjectives have to correspond to the gender and number of the noun or subject. The short form of letter ت, "ة" is suffixed to nouns and adjectives when the noun qualified is in the feminine gender, as is shown in the second sentence here.

The male doctor is present.	الطبيب حاضر
The lady doctor is present.	الطبيبة حاضرة

The addition of ة (the sign of feminine gender) in the second sentence is used both for the subject and the predicate. When the above sentences are used in the plural number both the subject and the predicate undergo vowel changes which is peculiar to the Arabic language.e.g:

The male doctors are present.	الاطباء حاضرون
The lady doctors are present	الطبيبات حاضرات

PRONOUNS: Pronouns are of two varieties,

(1) Those which are written separately e.g: هو *"he"* هي *"she"*,

انت *"you"* أنـا I (am)

Page 61 I am happy أنا سعيـد

Page 62 He is my brother هو أخي

(2) The second variety of pronouns are suffixed to

(a) either nouns e.g قلمه *"his pen"*. This also indicates possession.

(b) to verbs e,g: كتبته *"I wrote to him"*

(c) or suffixed to prepositions e,g: له *"for him"*.

DEMONSTRATIVE: Demonstrative pronouns which are used often are هذا "this" for near objects and ذلك "that" for distant objects. e.g:

page 32 This is a big market هذا سوق كبير

page 42 This is possible هذا ممكن

That is a factory ذلك مصنع

POSSESSION: Possession or ownership is conveyed in English by the use of apostrphe and s ('s) or by the use of preposition "of". In Arabic it is conveyed

1. By making suitable changes in the vowels, e.g:

the colour of the sky is blue لَونُ السماء أزرق

2. By suffixing possessive pronouns

(a) to nouns "قَلَمُهُ" *his pen*

(b) to verbs "كتبتُـهُ" *I wrote to him*

(c) to prepositions "لَـهُ" *for him.*

INTERROGATIVES: Some commonly used interrogatives are given here.

Page 15	هل تريد غرفة مفردة	(هل)
Page 33	كم الثمن؟	(كم)
Page 17	ما أوقات الفطور والغداء	(ما)
Page 37	أين محل الغسل	(أين)
Page 46	كيف حالك؟	(كيف)
Page 57	متى يفتح البنك؟	(متى)
Page 58	أي خدمة أخرى؟	(أي)
"Who is he"	من هو؟	مَن

PREPOSITIONS: The use of a preposition brings about vowel change, i.e., the noun that follows it is given ـِ (vowel "i")

Page 26	حضرت من الهند	(مِنْ)
Page 16	تفضل الي المدير	(الي)
Page 15	لاسبوع فقط	(ل)
Page 17	بالحليب	(ب)
Page 27	العمل في المصنع مريح	(في)
Page 27	عدد العمال فيه كثير	*(في+ه = فيه)
Page 18	ومطبخ مع فرن	(مَعَ)
Page 40	معه حقيبة	*(مع+ه = معه)

* a combination of preposition and pronoun

CONJUNCTIONS: Some conjunctions used in this book are;

Page 17	خبز وجبنة	(و)
Page 18	أريد بيت أو شقة	(أو)
Page 36	هل تريد باكمام طويلة ام قصيرة	(أم)

VERBS: There are three categories of verbs, الفعل الماضي (al fi'l al māḍi), past tense, الفعل المضارع (al fi'l al muḍari'), the present and future tense, الفعل الامر (al fi'l al amr), the imperative.

All these categories are spread over the lessons in this book. While studying the Arabic language through a teacher the student will get acquainted with verbal root and its derivatives and their conjugation. The conversion of a verb from the past tense to the future tense is done by vowel changes and the use of "ا ت ي ن".

The auxiliary verbs in the Arabic text have been sparingly used, they not only bring about changes in the vowels of the subject and the predicate but meaning too.

Past tense:	Page 7	وافق مدير الهجرة	(وافق)
	Page 6	قدمت له تفاصيل	(قدمت)
Future tense:	Page 6	الموظف يفحص الاوراق	(يفحص)
	Page 6	نطلب بعض المعلومات	(نطلب)
Imperative:	Page 10	خذ راحة	(خذ)
	Page 40	ادفع خمسة ريال	(ادفع)

Negative: The articles لا is often used to indicate the negative.

Page 1	لا أعرف القراءة والكتابة	(لا)
Page 36	لا بأس	(لا)

SENTENCE: There are two types of sentences in Arabic.

(1) The Verbal Sentence which starts with a verb e.g:

ذهب نبيل الي المدرسة *Nabeel went to the school.*

(2) The Nominal Sentence which starts with a subject followed by a predicate. e.g:

فاضل حاضر *Fadil is present*

This sentence is a complete sentence as it consists of a subject فاضل and a predicate حاضر, though the requirement of finite verb is apparently not found in it. The same rule applies to the following sentences on page 8

1. المطارمزدهم 2. التدخين ممنوع

COMPREHENSIVENESS: Arabic is such a comprehensive language that what looks like a word conveys the meaning of a complete sentence. The expression on page 48 أشكرك "I thank you" contains the three ingredients of a sentence, subject, verb and object.

ADDITIONAL VOCABULARY
in the English alphabetical order
with emphasis on Arabic words
which could be used in different contexts.

A

at, upon	'alā	علـي
able, competent	qādir	قادر
ablution for prayer	wuḍu´	وضـوء
abnormal, unnatural	ḡair ṭabī'i	غير طبيعي
abolish, to cancel	fasaka	فسخ
abortion, abrogation	isqāṭ	إسقاط
about, according to	ḥaula - 'an	حول – عن
above, on	fauq	فوق
abroad, out of country	kārij al bilād	خارج البلاد
abrogation,cancellation	ilḡā´	اِلْغَاء
absence, being away	ḡiyāb	غياب
absent, unseen	ḡāib	غائب
absolutely,	'alā al iṭlāq	علـي الاطـلاق
abstract, extract,gist	kulāsa	خـلاصة
absurd,silly,rediculous	sakīf	سخـيـف
abundant,many,much	katīr	كثير

academy	academīa	أكادمية
acceptable,satisfactory	maqbūl	مقبول
acceptance, approval	qabūl	قبول
accident,mishap,event	ḥādiṯa	حادثة
accommodation,house	maskan	مسكن
accord,agreement	ittifāq	إتفاق
account,bill,invoice	ḥisāb	حساب
account (Current)	ḥisāb jāri	حساب جار
accountability	muḥāsaba	محاسبة
accountable person,	mas'ūl	مسئول
accountant, auditor	muḥāsib	محاسب
accredited, agent	mufawwaḍ	مفوض
accumulation,	tajammu'	تجمع
accuracy, fineness	diqqa	دقة
accurate,exact,correct	maḍbūt	مضبوط
accusation,charge	tuhma	تهمة
ache, pain, ailment	waja' - alam	وجع/ ألم
achievement,	injāz	إنجاز
acid, sour	ḥāmiḍ	حامض
acknowledgement,	i'tirāf	إعتراف
acquire,get,to recover	ḥaṣala	حصل

acquisition,attainment	taḥsīl	تحصيل
across,to cross, pass	'abara	عبر
act, action	'amal	عمل
active, cheerful, gay	nashīṭ	نشيط
actor, agent,	mummaṯil	ممثل
actress,	mummaṯila	ممثلة
actual,real,authentic	ḥaqīqī	حقيقي
actually, in fact	fi al wāqi'	في الواقع
acute,severe,forceful	shadīd	شديد
add, to attach	aḍāfa	أضاف
addition,increment,	ziyāda	زيادة
address,heading,sign	'unwān	عنوان
adequate,fitting	munāsib	مناسب
adhesive,affixed,	mulṣaq	ملصق
administrative	idāri	إداري
administrator,Director	mudīr	مدير
admire, to wonder	a'ja ba	أعجب
admission, entry	idḵāl	إدخال
adult, legally major	bāliḡ	بالغ
advance, progress	taqaddum	تقدم
advancement, progress	nahḍa	نهضة

advantage, profit	fāida	فائدة
adventure	muḡāmara	مغامرة
advertisement,	i'lān - nashar	إعلان / نشر
advice,	naṣīḥa	نصيحة
advise, to guide	naṣaḥa	نصح
advocate	muḥām - wakīl	محام / وكيل
aerodrome	maṭār	مطار
aeroplane	ṭayyāra	طيارة
affair, problem	mas'ala	مسئلة
affected, influenced by	muta'ṯar	متأثر
alliance, pact	ḥalf	حلف
affidavit	iqrār kitābi	إقرار كتابي
affluent, rich	ḡani	غني
afraid, fearful	ḵāif	خائف
afternoon	ba'd al-zuhar	بعد الظهر
afterwards	ba'd ḏālik	بعد ذلك
agree, to approve	wāfaqa	وافق
agreement, approval	muwāfaqa	موافقة
agriculture	zirā'a	زراعة
aim,goal,objective	hadaf	هدف
alarm, warning	inḏār	إنذار

alchemy	al kīmiyā'	الكيمياء
alcohol	kuḥūl	كحول
alien, foreigner	ajnabi	أجنبي
all, entire, whole	jamī'	جميع
allowance, increase	'ilāwa	علاوات
alone, detached	munfaridan	منفردا
alteration, change	taġīr	تغيير
alternatively	bil-tabādul	بالتبادل
always, ever	dā'iman	دائما
ambassador	safīr	سفير
ambiguity	ibhām	إبهام
ambulance	'araba mustashfa	عربة مستشفي
ambulance service	is'āf	إسعاف
amity, friendship	ṣadāqa	صداقة
amount, extent, range	mablaġ	مبلغ
ample, abundant	wāfir	وافر
analysis	taḥlīl	تحليل
anarchy, disorder	fawḍa	فوضى
angle	zāwiya	زاوية
angry, furious	ġaḍbān	غضبان
animal	ḥayawān	حيوان

animating, refreshing	mun'ish	منعش
animosity,hatred	buḡḍ	بغض
anniversary	'id sanawi	عيد سنوي
announce, to disclose	'alana	أعلن
annual, yearly	sanawi	سنوي
another,not,non-,un-,	ḡair	غير
answer,reply,response	jawāb	جواب
antecedents,	sawābiq	سوابق
anthem, national song	nashiṭ waṭani	نشيط وطني
antibiotic	muḍād lil jarāsim	مضاد للجراثيم
anticipation,expectation	tawaqqu'	توقع
antique, ancient	'atīq	عتيق
anxiety, perplexity	ḥīra	حِيرة
anybody	ayy insān	أي إنسان
anyhow,at any extent	'ala kulli ḥāl	على كل حال
apartment	shaqqa	شَقّـة
apology, excuse	i'tiḏār	إعتذار
apostle, messenger	rasūl	رسـول
appeal, seeking refuge	iltijā	إلتجـاء
appearance,exterior	maẓhar	مظهر
appendix, attache	mulḥaq	ملحق

applicable, in agreement with	muṭābiq	مطابق
applicant, claimant	muqaddim al-ṭalab	مقدم الطلب
application,demand	ṭalab	طلب
appointment,employment	tawẓīf	توظيف
apprentice,under trial	taḥt al-tamrīn	تحت التمرين
appropriate,suitable	lā'iq	لائق
approval, consent	muwāfaqa	موافقة
approximately,nearly	taqrīban	تقريبا
aptitude, capacity	liyāqa	لياقة
arabic language	al luḡa al ʻarabiya	اللغة العربية
architect (engineering)	muhandis ma'māri	مهندس معماري
area,floor space,extent	misāḥa	مساحة
argue, to discuss	nāqasha	ناقش
army	jaish	جيش
arrange,to set,regulate	rattaba,naẓẓama	رتب / نظم
arrears of salary, rent	muta'ak̲k̲arat	متأخرات
arrival, receipt	wuṣūl	وصول
art, special field	fann	فنّ
article,clause,matter	mādda	مادة
artificial,synthetic	ṣanāi'ī	صناعي

artist,craftsman	fannān	فنّان
ascertain,to make sure	a'kkada	أكّد
ask, to question	sa'la	سأل
asleep	nāi'm	نائم
aspire, to desire	ishtāqa	إشتاق
assemble,to gather	ijtamaa'a	إجتمع
assignment, appointing agent	tawkīl	توكيل
association,society	jam'īya	جمعية
astonished,amazed	mundahish	مندهش
at, in, on	fī, 'inda, 'alā	في / عند / على
at first	awwalan	أولا
at least	'alā al aqall	علي الأقل
at once, immediately	ḥālan	حالا
ate, to eat	akala	أكل
atlas	aṭlas	أطلس
atmosphere, space	jaww	جو
attach, to stick	alṣaqa	ألصق
attempt, effort, try	muḥāwala	محاولة
attend, to be present	ḥaḍara	حضر
attendance,participation	ḥuḍūr	حضور

attention,inclination	iltifāt	إلتفات
attestation,endorsement	taṣdīq	تصديق
attorney authorised agent	wakīl mufawwaḍ	وكيل مفوض
attorney power, delegation of authority	tafwīḍ	تفويض
attractive,charming	jaḏḏāb	جذّاب
auction	mazād - ḥarāj	مزاد / حراج
audience,gathering	ijtimāa'	إجتماع
audio	simāi'	سماعي
auditor (of accounts)	fāḥis al ḥisābāt	فاحص الحسابات
auditorium,hall	qā'a	قاعة
author, writer	muṣannif	مصنف
authority, power,	sulṭa	سلطة
automatic	automatiki	أوطوماتيكي
available, present	mawjūd	موجود
average, middle,	mutawassaṭ	متوسّط
aviator, pilot	ṭayyār	طيار
avoid, to keep away	ijtanaba	إجتنب
awake, to get up	istayqada	إستيقظ
away, far, distant	ba'īd	بعيدا

B

bachelor, unmarried	'azab	عذب
bachelor of Arts	bakalōriyūs	بكلوريـوس
bachelor of science	bakalōriyūs 'ulūm	بكالوريوس علوم
back, behind	k̲alf	خلف
bacteria	baktīriya	بكتيريا
bad, useless	raddi	ردي
bag, purse, sack	kīs	كيـس
bail, guarantor	ḍāmin	ضامن
baker	k̲abbāz	خبـاز
bakery	mak̲baz	مخبز
balance,scales,justice	mīzān	ميزان
ball, globe	kurra	كرة
ban, prohibitted	mamnū'	ممنوع
bandage, dressing	'iṣāb	عصـاب
bangle	siwār	سوار
banishment, exile	nafy	نفي
bankrupt, insolvent	muflis	مفلس
banner, flag	'alam	علم
barber	ḥallāq	حلاق

bargaining	musāwama	مساومة
baren, sterile	'aqīm - 'aāqir	عقيم / عاقر
barrier,screen,hurdle	ḥājiz	حاجز
basic,main,essential	asāsi	أساسي
bathe, to wash	ḡasala	غسل
battery	baṭṭāriya	بطارية
battle, war	qitāl	قتال
bay, gulf	k̲alīj	خليج
be, was	kāna	كان
bare with, to tolerate	iḥtamala	إحتمل
beard	liḥya	لحية
beat, to strike	ḍaraba	ضرب
beautiful, lovely, pretty	jamīl	جميل
become	aṣbaha - ṣāra	أصبح – صار
because of	bi sabab	بسبب
bed	farsha - sarir	فرشة
bed spread	firāsh	فراش
bedouin	badawī	بدوي
befitting,suitable	munāsib	مناسب
before	qabl	قبل
befriend, to become friend	ṣādaqa	صادق

began, to start	bad'a - shara'a	بدأ / شرع
beggar, questioner	sā'il	سائل
beginner,novice	mubtadi'	مبتدئ
behaviour, conduct	sulūk	سلوك
behind, at the back	ḵalf	خلف
being, existence	wujūd	وجود
believe, to approve	ṣaddaqa	صدّق
bell	jaras	جرس
belongings,	mumtalākat	ممتلكات
belt	ḥizām	حزام
belt (safety)	ḥizām al amn	حزام الأمن
bend, to incline, tilt	mālā	مال
benefactor,charitable	muḥsin	محسن
beneficial,useful	nāfi'	نافع
beneficiary,deserving	mustaḥiq	مستحق
bereavement,	ḥirmān	حرمان
bestow, to grant	manaḥa - wahaba	منح/وهب
betray, to be disloyal	ḵana - ḡadara	خان / غدر
bidder at an auction	muzābid	مزابد
bigoted, fanatic	muta'aṣib	متعصب

bill, invoice	kashf ḥisāb	كشف حساب
blame, to scold	lowm	لوم
blank,not busy,vacant	fāriḡ	فارغ
bleed	sāla al-dam	سال الدم
blessing	baraka	بركة
blunt, not sharp	ḡair ḥād	غير حاد
boarding, offering food	taqdeem al akl	تقديم الاكل
boiler, cooking kettle	mirjal	مرجل
bold, courageous	shujāa'	شجاع
bomb, grenade	qumbula	قنبلة
bone	'azm	عظم
book	kitāb	كتاب
book seller	bāi' kutub	بائع كتب
borrow loan or a thing	iqtaraḍa	اقترض
botany	'ilm al-nabāt	علم النبات
both of them	kilāhuma	كلاهما
bottle, piece of glass	zujāja	زجاجة
boundless,unlimited	ḡair maḥdūd	غير محدود
boycott, break with	muqāt'aa	مقاطعة
branch of tree or institution	far'	فرع

breach, to break	kasr	كسر
bread	ḵubz	خبز
breadth	'arḍ	عرض
bribe, corruption	rushwa	رشوة
bride	'arūsa	عروسة
bride groom	'arīs	عريس
bridge, link	jisr	جسر
brief, extract	mulaḵḵas	ملخص
bright, shining	lāmi'	لامع
bring on, to fetch	jalaba - aḥḍara	جلب / أحض
broad, extensive	wāsi'	واسع
broadcasting of news, telecast	iḏā'a	إذاعة
broken, fractured	maksur	مكسور
broker commission agent	dallāl	دلال
brush for painting, tooth brush	fursha	فرشة
bucket	dalw	دلـــــو
budget, balance	mīzāniya	ميزانية
build, to construct	banā	بنى
building,construction	binā' - 'imāra	بناء / عمارة

bullet	raṣṣaṣa	رصاصة
burden, load	ṯaql	ثقل
burial	dafn	دفن
burn, to set fire	ḥaraqa	حرق
busy, occupied	mashḡūl	مشغول
buy, to purchase	ishtarā	اشترى

C

cabinet, room	ḡurfa	غرفـــــة
cable, wire	silk	ســلك
calamity, tragedy	kāriṯa	كارثة
calculate, to count	ḥasaba	حسب
calcuation, arithmetic	ḥisāb	حساب
calender of Gregorian or Hijra era	taqwīm	تقويم
call, appeal	nidā' - ṭalab	نداء / طلب
cancel, to abrogate	abṭala	أبطل
candidate for job or election	murashaḥ	مرشح
candle, wax candle	sham'a	شمعة
caravan, convoy	qāfila	قافلة
cardiac, pertaining to the heart	qalbī	قلبـي

care, regard,attention	'ināya	عناية
career,profession,trade	ḥirfa	حرفة
careless, neglectful	muhmil	مهمل
cargo, load	shaḥna	شحنة
carry, to transport	ḥamala-intaqala	حمل / انقل
carve out, to engrave	naqasha	نقش
case,situation,state	ḥāl	حال
cash, ready money	naqd	نقد
cashier,money changer	ṣarrāf	صراف
cause, problem	qaḍīya	قضية
caution, carefulness	iḥtiyāṭ	إحتياط
celebration, festival	iḥtifāl	احتفال
censorship, control	riqaba	رقابة
central, - administration	markazi	مركزي
ceremony	ḥafla	حفلة
certificate,witness	shhāda	شهادة
challenge, to oppose	taḥadda	تحدّ
chamber of commerce	ḡurfa al-tijāra	غرفة التجارة
change, replacement	tabaddul	تبدل
character, (morals)	k̲ulq	خلق
charity, good words	iḥsan	إحسان

chart, map	ḵarīṭa	خريطـة
chemistry	al kīmīya'	الكيميـاء
chew	maḍaḡa	مضغ
chief,director,president	mudīr - ra'īs	مدير / رئيس
choice, selection	iḵtiyār	إختيار
choose, to elect	intaḵaba	انتخب
christian	masīḥī	مسيحي
circle, range, extent	dā'ira	دائرة
circumcision`	ḵitan	ختان
circumstances, conditions	ẓurūf	ظروف
citizen,countryman	muwāṭin	مواطن
civilian, town dweller	madani	مدني
clause of contract,	band	بند
clean, neat, tidy	naẓīf	نظيف
clear, obvious, evident	wāḍih	واضح
clerk, writer	kātib	كاتب
clever, cunning	shāṭir	شاطر
climate, weather	ṭaqs	طقس
climb, to ascent	tasallaqa	تسلق
cling to, paste	iltaṣaqa	التصـق
clinic	'iyāda	عيـادة

clock	sā'a	ساعة
close, end	nihāya	نهاية
closure,cancellation	iḡlāq	إغـلاق
clue,telephone directory	dalīl	دليل
coincide, agreement	ittifāq	اتفـاق
colleague, companion	zamīl	زميل
collect, to gather	jamma'a	جمّـع
college	kulliya	كليـة
collision,clash,impact	taṣādum	تصادم
colony, settlement	musta'mara	مسـتعمرة
colour	lawn	لون
comb	mushṭ	مشط
combine, to mix	mazaja	مزج
come	jā' - atā'	جاء / أتى
commence, to start	ibtadā'-bashara	ابتـدأ / باشر
comment, to explain	fassara	فسّـر
commerce, trade	tijāra	تجارة
committee,	lajna	لجنة
commodity,merchandise	biḍā'a	بضاعة
correspondence	murāsala	مراسلة
companion, friend	rafīq	رفيق

company,	sharika	شركة
compare,to put together	qārana	قارن
compel, to use force	ajbara	أجبر
compensation	ta'wīḍ	تعويض
complaint	shakwa	شكوة
competent, expert	māhir	ماهر
complete, to perfect	akmala	أكمل
component, made up	murakkab	مركب
compulsory,necessary	lāzim	لازم
conceal, to hide	katama	كتم
concerning,regarding	min k̲uṣūs	من خصوص
condition,clause	sharṭ	شـرط
conduct,behaviour	sīra	سيرة
confession,recognition	i'tirāf	اعتراف
congratulation	mubārak	مبارك
connection, relation	ilāqa	علاقة
conscience	damīr	ضمير
consequence,result	natīja	نتيجة
consignee	al mustalim	المستلم
constitution,law, rule	dastūr-nizām	دستور / نظام
consult, to seek advice	shawara	شاور

consultant, adviser	mustashār	مستشار
continue	istamarra	استمر
contract, agreement	'aqd - ittifāqiya	عقد / اتفاقية
control, authority	idāra - sulṭa	إدارة / سلطة
converse, to talk	takallama-ḥadaṯa	تكلم/حادث
cook	ṭabbāḵ	طباخ
co-operate, to assist	'aawana	عاون
could make possible	amkana	أمكن
courage, bravery	shujā'a	شجاعة
court, tribunal	maḥkama	محكمة
coward	jabbān	جبان
crane, lifting apparatus	rāfi'	رافع
create, to make	ḵalaqa - awjada	خلق / أوجد
credit, loan	qarḍ	قرض
crescent, new moon	hilāl	هلال
crime, harm, wrong	jarīma	جريمة
criminal, culprit	mujrim	مجرم
criticise, to evaluate	naqada	نقد
cross	ṣalīb	صليب
crossing,transit,	'ubūr	عبور
crude, raw	ḵām	خام

cruel, severe, harsh	'anīf	عنيف
cry, shout, weeping	bakā - ṣaraḵ	بكاء / صرخ
culture, civilization	ṯaqāfa	ثقافة
currency	'umla dārija	عملة دارجة
current	tayyār	تيـار
current account	ḥisāb jāri	حساب جار
custom dues	rusūm al jumruk	رسوم الجمرك
cut off, to cut in two	qaṭṭa'a	قطّـع

D

daily	kull yawm	كل يوم
damage, harm	ḍarara	ضـرر
dancing	raqṣ	رقـص
darkness, gloom	ẓulma	ظلمة
date	tārīḵ	تاريخ
date fruit	tamr	تمـر
dead (died)	mātā	مات
deaf	aṭrash	أطـرش
debit, debt, liability	dain	ديـن
deceit, crook, cheat	ḵadāa'	خداع
deduct, to drop, to fall	asqaṭa	أسقط

deep, profound	'amīq	عميق
deficit, loss, shortage	naqṣ	نقص
degree, status	daraja - rutba	درجة / رتبة
delegate,repreṣentative	mandūb	مندوب
deliver, to hand over	sallama	سلم
demand, claim	ṭalab	طلب
dentist	ṭabīb asnān	طبيب أسنان
department	idāra	إدارة
deposit, to save	ḏaḵara	ذخر
depot, warehouse	mustauda'	مستودع
describe	waṣafa	وصف
desert	ṣaḥrā'	صحراء
desire, wish	raǧba	رغبة
detailed statement	tafṣīl	تفصيل
diagnosis,identification	tashḵīs	تشخيص
dialogue,conversation	mḥadaṯa	محادثة
difference, division	farq	فرق
difficult, hard	ṣ'aab	صعب
disappointment,failure	fashl	فشل
discount, rebate	ḵaṣam	خصم
discover, to uncover	kashafa	كشف

disgrace,humiliation	faḍīḥa	فضيحة
dispute, strife	nizā'	نزاع
dissatisfied	ḡair rāḍi	غير راض
distance	masāfa	مسافة
distinguished,excellent	mumtāz	ممتاز
distribution	tauzī'	توزيع
disunity, separation	infiṣāl	انفصال
do a thing, perform	fa'ala	فعل
document, record	waṯīqa	وثيقة
doubt, suspicion	rayb - shak	ريب / شك
down, below, under	taḥat	تحت
draft, money order	hawala maliya	حوالة مالية
drainage, water course	majāri'	مجاري
draw, to draw from bank	saḥaba	سحب
drawing, picture	rasm - taṣwīr	رسم / تصوير
dream	manām - ḥulm	منام / حلم
dress, clothes, garment	libās - ridā'	لباس / رداء
drink	shariba	شرب
drive a vehicle	siyāqa	سياقة
dry	jāff - yābis	جاف / يابس
due, claim, right	ḥaqq - dain	حق / دين

duplicate copy	nuska̲	نسخة
duty, obligatory	wājib - farḍ	واجب / فرض
dynamo	dynamo	دينامو

E

easy, smooth, soft	sahal	سهل
eat, to consume	akala	اكل
economics	iqtiṣād	إقتصاد
education	ta'līm	تعليم
effect, result	natīja	نتيجة
efficient, capable	qadīr	قدير
effort, attempt	majhūd	مجهود
eject, to send out	ak̲raja	أخرج
election,selection	intik̲āb	إنتخاب
electricity	kahrabā'	كهرباء
electronic	elektroni	إلكتروني
element	'unṣur	عنصر
emancipate, to free	ḥarrara	حرّر
embargo, prevention	manu' - ḥaẓr	منع / حظر
embassy of a country	ṣafāra	سفارة

misappropriation	iḵtilās	إختـلاس
emergency situation	al-ṭawāri	الطـوارئ
emigrant	muhājir	مهـاجر
employee,worker,officer	muwazzaf	موظف
employer	mustaḵdim	مستخدم
employment,utilization	istiḵdām	إستخـدام
empty	fāriġ	فارغ
encashment, money changing	ṣarafa	صرف
encourage	shajjaa'	شجّع
end,cease,closure	intihā'	إنتهاء
enemy	'adūw	عـدو
enforce, to make compulsory	alzama	ألزم
engaged in, busy with	mushtaġal fi	مشـتغل في
engineer	muhandis	مهندس
engineering	handasa	هندسـة
enhance, to increase	zāda	زاد
enjoin, lay condition	ishtaraṭa	إشترط
enjoyment,pleasure	istimtā'	استمتـاع
enter, to include	daḵala	دخل

entitled to, deserving	mustaḥiqq	مستحق
entry, admission	duk̲ūl	دخول
epidemic	wabā'	وباء
equality, equal right	musāwa	مساواة
equipment, implements	mu'addāt	معدّات
erring, mistaken	ḡalṭān	غلطان
error, mistake	ḡaliṭa	غلط
escape, to flee	farra	فرّ
especial, private possession	k̲uṣūsi	خصوصي
essence	jawhar - lubb	جوهر / لب
establish, to set up	anshā'	أنشأ
establishment, firm	mu'assasa	مؤسسة
estate (property)	'aqār	عقار
estimation, apprisal	taqdīr	تقدير
eternal	abadi	أبدي
ethics, character	ak̲lāq	اخلاق
evacuate, to unload	afraḡa	أفرغ
evaluate, to estimate	qaddara	قدّر
even, till	ḥatta	حتى
event, development	waqi'a	واقعة

ever, never	abadan	أبـدا
eviction	ik̲rāj	إخراج
evidence,certificate	shahāda	شـهادة
evil, wrong	shar	شر
examination, test	imtiḥān	إمتحان
example,pattern,sample	namūz̲aj	نموذج
exceed, surplus	ziyada	زيادة
exception,exclusion	istithna'	إستثناء
exchange, pay office	maṣrif	مصرف
excise, tax, levy	ḍarība	ضريبـة
exclude,prevent,to stop	manaa'	منـع
excuse, pardon	ma'd̲ira	معذرة
executive	tanfīd̲i	تنفيذي
execute, to complete a work, to fulfil	anjaza	أنجز
exempt, excluded	mustat̲na'	مستثنـى
exercise, practice	tamrīn	تمريـن
exhibition,show room	ma'raḍ	معرض
existence,being,presence	wujūd	وجود
exit, departure	ḳurūj	خروج
expand, to extend	imtadda	إمتـدّ
expansion, extension	tamdīd	تمديـد

expect, wait intaẓara - tawaqqa'a		انتظر/توقع
expense,cost,outlay	nafaqa	نفقة
experience,knowledge	k̲ibra	خبرة
expert, experienced	k̲abīr	خبير
expiration,close, termination	intihā'	إنتهاء
export, despatch	taṣdīr	تصدير
extend, renewal	ittasa' - tajdīd	اتسع / تجديد
external,foreign,outside	k̲ariji	خارجي
extra, increase	ziyāda	زيادة
extraordinary	ḡair 'aādi	غير عادي
extremely, much	jiddan	جدّا

F

facility,convenience	sahūla	سهولة
fact, reality	haqīqa	حقيقة
factory	maṣna'a	مصنع
fail, to be unsuccessful	fashala	فشل
faith, belief	imān	ايمان
fall, dropping	suqūṭ	سقوط
false, lying	kād̲ib	كاذب
fame, reputation	shuhra	شهرة

famine	qaḥaṭ	قحط
far off	ba'īdan	بعيدا
farewell	wadā'	وداع
fasting	ṣiyām	صيام
fate, fortune	ḥaẓẓ - bakt	حظّ / بخت
faulty, defective	nāqiṣ	ناقص
favour,charity,goodness	iḥsān	إحسان
fear, dread	k̲awf	خوف
fee, tax	rasm	رسم / رسوم
feel,to sense	aḥassa	أحسّ
female	unt̲a	أنثى
festival, carnival	mahrajān	مهرجان
filled, full	malī'	ملئ
financial	māli	مالي
find, to get, to meet	wajada	وجد
fine, penalty	ḡarāma	غرامة
fire	ḥarīqa - nār	حريقة
firm,commercial company	sharika	شركة
first aid	is'āf awwali	إسعاف أوّل
fit, proper, suitable	munāsib	مناسب
fix, errect	naṣaba	نصب

fixed, stable	ṯābit	ثابت
flat in a building	shaqqa	شقة
fluid	sā'il	سائل
food, diet	ta'ām	طعام
force, power	quwwa - qudra	قدرة / قوة
forget	nasiya	نسي
forgive, to excuse	sāmaḥa	سامح
formal, official	rasmī	رسمي
foundry	masbak	مسبك
free, independent	ḥurr	حرّ
fresh, new	ṭāzij	طازج
full, filled up	mumtali'	ممتلئ
fund, amount	mablaḡ	مبلغ
funeral procession,bier	jināza	جنازة
furniture	aṯāṯ	أثاث

G

gain, profit	ribḥ	ربح
game, sports, play	la'b	لعب
garden	ḥadīqa	حديقة
gas	ḡāz	غاز

gather, to collect	tajjamma'a	تجمّع
gender, sex, sort	jins	جنس
generator	muwallid	مولّد
generous, noble	karīm	كريم
genius,ingenious person	'abqarī	عبقري
genuine, original	aṣli	أصلي
germ	jarṯuma	جرثومة
get, to receive	ḥasala - nāla	حصل / نال
give, offer	'atā	أعطى
go, to depart	ḏahaba	ذهب
gold	ḏahab	ذهبْ
goal , aim	hadaf	هدف
good thing, benefit welfare	ḵair	خير
goods, commodities	biḍā'a	بضاعة
government	ḥukuma	حكومة
governer, ruler, judge	ḥākim	حاكم
grade, status	daraja	درجة
graduate of university	ḵirrij jāmi'a	خريج جامع
grand, mighty	'azīm	عظيم
grant, donation	minḥa	منحة

gratuity, gift	'atīya	عطية
grave	qabr	قبر
greed, ambition	ṭama'	طمع
greeting, salutation	taḥiyya	تحية
grief, sorrow	ḥuzn	حزن
group, association	jamā'a	جماعـة
grow, breed	nabata	نبت
guarantee, surity	ḍaman	ضمـان
guarantor, sponsor	kafīl	كفيـل
guard, watchman	ḥāris	حارس
guest	ḍaif	ضيف
gulf	ḵalīj	خليج
gum	ṣamḡ	صمـغ
gun	bunduqīya	بندقية

H

habit, custom, practice	'āada	عـادة
hair	sha'r	شعر
hall, auditorium	qā'aa	قاعة
halt, stopping place	waqūf	وقوف
hammer	miṭraqa	مطرقة

hand bag	shanṭa	شـنطة
handkerchief	mindīl	منديل
handsome, pleasant	laṭīf	لطيف
happy, lucky	sa'aīd	سـعيد
harbour, port	mīna'	ميناء
hard, unpolished	k̲ashin	خشن
hard currency	'umla ṣaba'	عملة صعبة
harmful, damaging	muḍir	مضر
haste, speed	sur'a	سرعة
hate, dislike	karāhiya	كراهية
he	huwa	هو
health	ṣiḥḥa	صحة
hear, to listen	sami'a	سمع
hebrew	'ibrāṇi	عبراني
heavy, burdensome	t̲aqīl	ثقيـل
height, elevation	irtifā'	إرتفاع
help, assistance	musā'ada	مسـاعدة
hero, brave	baṭal	بطل
hiding, disappearance	ik̲tifā'	إختفاء
high, top quality	'alin	عالٍ
hindi	al luġa al hindiya	اللغة الهندية

hindu	hindūki	هندوكي
hire, rent	ujra	أجرة
history	'ilm al-tārīk̲	علم التاريخ
holy, sacred	muqaddas	مقدس
home, landing place	manzil	منزل
hope, expectation	amal	أمل
hospital	mustashfā	مستشفى
host	mudif	مضيف
hostage, mortgage	rahīna	رهينة
housewife	rabbat al bait	ربة البيت
human being	insān	إنسان
humidity, wetness	ruṭuba	رطوبة
hunger	jū'	جوع
hygiene, health care	ḥifẓ al-ṣiḥḥa	حفظ الصحة
hypocrite	munāfiq	منافق

I

I	anā	أنا
ice	t̲alj	ثلج
idea, opinion	fikr	فكر
identity, identity card	huwiya	هوية

idle, lazy	kasūl	كسول
ignorant	jāhil	جاهل
ill, sick	marīḍ	مريض
illegal, prohibited	ḥarām	حرام
immature, not ripe	ḡair nāḍij	غير ناضج
immediate, urgent	musta'jil	مستعجل
immigration	muhājara	مهاجرة
immorality, indecent	faḥush	فحش
immunity	ḥaṣāna	حصانة
impartial, just person	munṣif	منصف
imperfect, faulty	nāqiṣ	ناقص
implore, to request	iltamasa	التمس
import	istīrād	استيراد
importance,significance	ahammiya	أهمية
important, significant	muhimm	مهم
impossible	mustaḥīl	مستحيل
improper, not suitable	ḡair munāsib	غير مناسب
improve,to show progress	taḥassana	تحسّن
impure, not clean	ḡair naqīy	غير نقي
inability, weakness	'ajz	عجز
inactive,lazy	kaslān	كسلان

inauguration, opening	iftitāḥ	إفتتاح
incense	baḵūr	بخور
incident, event	ḥādiṯa	حادثة
including, containing	mushtamil	مشتمل
income, revenue	daḵal	دخل
income tax	ḍarība(t) al-daḵal	ضريبة الدخل
incompetent, unfit	ḡair qādir	غير قادر
incomplete, imperfect	ḡair kāmil	غير كامل
inconsistent, not firm	ḡair ṯābit	غير ثابت
increase, addition	ziyāda	زيادة
increment,extra allowance,	'ilāwa	علاوة
indeed, in fact	fi al ḥaqīqa	في الحقيقة
indemnity,compensation	ta'wīḍ	تعويض
indicate, make clear	awḍaḥ	أوضح
indirect	ḡair mubāshir	غير مباشر
individual,single,one	fard	فرد
industry	ṣinā'aa	صناعة
infancy, childhood	ṭufūla	طفولة
inferior, lower	asfal	أسفل
influence, effect	ta'ṯīr	تأثير
information, news	ḵabar	خبر

ingredients, contents	al-tarkīb	التركيب
inhabitant, residing	muqīm	مقيم
inherit, to be heir	waraṯa	ورث
initial, elementary	ibtidā'i	إبتدائي
injure, wound	jaraḥa	جرح
injustice, unfair	ẓulm	ظلم
ink	ḥibr	حبر
innocent, not guilty	barī'	برئ
innovation	bida'	بدعة
inoculation	taṭ'īim	تطعيم
inquiry,information office	isti'lām	إستعلام
insane mad	majnūn	مجنون
insecurity, unsafe	'adm amān	عدم أمان
inside	dākil	داخل
insist, to persist	aṣarra 'alā	أصر علي
insomnia, sleeplessness	araq	أرق
inspect, to check	fattasha	فتّش
instalment	qisṭ	قسط
instead of	badlan min	بدلا من
institution,	m'ahad	معهد
instrument	āla	آلة

insult, abuse	ihāna	إهانة
insurance,security	ta'mīn	تأمين
integrity, honesty	istiqāma	إستقامة
intellect, reason	'aql	عقل
intend, to pursue	qaṣada	قصد
intention, objective	ḡarḍ	غرض
interest, gain	ribḥ	ربح
interference, entry	tadak̲k̲al	تدخّل
interior,inward,home	dāk̲ili	داخلي
intermediate,middle	mutawassiṭ	متوسط
international	duwali	دولي
interpreter, translator	mutarjim	مترجم
interval, period	fatra	فترة
interview,meeting	muqābala	مقابلة
intrigue, trick	makīda	مكيدة
introduction,presenting	taqdīm	تقديم
invalid, cancelled	lāḡin	لاغٍ
invention	ik̲tirā'	إختراع
investigate, to examine medically	faḥasa	فحص
invitation, calling up	da'wwa	دعوة
invoice	fātura	فاتورة

Islamic religion	al islām	الاسلام
isolate, to separate	'azala	عزل
issue, problem	mas'ala	مسألة
itinerary, traveller's programme	dalīl al musāfir	دليل المسافر

J

jail	sijn	سجن
jealousy, envy	ḥasad	حسد
jews	al hūd	الهود
job, labour	'amal	عمل
joining, gathering	jam'a	جمع
joke, make fun	mazaḥa	مزح
journal, news paper	jarīda	جريدة
joy, festival	faraḥ	فرح
judge, magistrate	qāḍin	قاضٍ
jump, leap	qafaza	قفز
jungle	ḡaba	غابة
justice, fairness	'adl	عدل

K

keeping, custody	hifẓ	حفظ

kerchief	mindīl	منديل
kernel, core, essence	lubb	لـبّ
key	miftāḥ	مفتاح
kidnap, pluck	k̠aṭafa	خطـف
kill	qatala	قتـل
kind, charitable	muḥsin	محسن
king	malik	ملك
knife	sikkin	سكين
knock	daqqa	دقّ
know, to recognize	'arafa	عرف
knowledge, science	'ilm	علم
known, sure	ma'lūm	معلوم

L

laboratory	muk̠tabar	مختبر
labourer, worker	'aāmil	عامل
lack, shortage, deficit	naqṣ	نقص
ladder	sullam	سلّم
lady, Mrs.	al-sayida	السيدة
lady cook	ṭabbak̠a	طبّاخة
lame, limping	a'raj	أعرج

lamp, light	miṣbāḥ	مصباح
land, country	bilād	بلاد
language	luḡa	لغة
large, big, spacious	kabīr	كبير
last, finally	aḵīran	أخيرا
late, lagging behind	muta'aḵḵir	متأخر
laugh	ḍaḥika	ضحك
laundryman, washer	ḡassāl	غسّال
law, constitution	qānūn	قانون
lawful, permitted	ḥalāl	حلال
lawyer, advocate	muḥām	محام
lazy, inactive	kaslān	كسلان
leader, commander	qā'id	قائد
league, association	'aṣba	عصبة
learn, to study	darasa	درس
leasing, rent	ijāra	إجارة
leather, skin, hide	jild	جلد
leave, permit, licence	ruḵṣa	رخصة
ledger	daftar al ḥisāb	دفتر الحساب
left side	yusrā	يسرى
leisure, empty	farāḡ	فراغ

lend, to loan	aqraḍa	أقرض
length, height	ṭūl	طول
letter, message	risāla	رسالة
liberty, freedom	ḥurriya	حرية
lid, covering, wrap	gita'	غطاء
life, life blood	ḥayāh	حيـاة
lift, elevator	miṣ'ad	مصعد
light, lamp	nūr	نور
light weight, thin	ḵafīf	خفيف
likeness, similar	mitl	مثل
like, I love	uḥibbu	أحب
likely, possible	mumkin	ممكن
limited, bounded	maḥdūd	محدود
linkage, junction, union	waṣl	وصل
listen, to hear	istami'	إستمع
literature	al adab	الأدب
livelihood,way of living	ma'īsha	معيشـة
load, cargo, shipment	shaḥn	شحن
loan, liability	dain	ديـن
local, native	maḥalli	محلّي
lock	qufl	قفل

look, to see, watch	naẓara	نظر
loss, damage	ḵasāra	خسارة
lost, missing	mafqūd	مفقود
love, affection	hubb	حبّ
loyal, trustworthy	amīn	أمين
lucky, fortunate	muwaffaq	موفق
luggage, necessities of life	matā'	متاع
lunar, moon like	qamari	قمري
lust, passion	shahwa	شهوة
luxury, affluence	taraf	ترف

M

machine	makina	مكنة
mad, insane	majnūn	مجنون
magazine, store, shop	maḵzan	مخزن
maiden, girl	fatāh	فتاة
mail, post	barīd	بريد
maintenance of machine	ṣiyāna	صيانة
make, to manufacture	ṣana'a	صنع
maker, manufacturer	ṣāni'	صانع
male	ḏakar	ذكر

malice, hatred	ḥiqd	حقد
man	rajul	رجل
management administration	idāra	أدار
manager, director	mudīr	مدير
manifest, clear	ẓāhir	ظاهر
manifold, numerous	'adīd	عديـد
mankind, people	nās	ناس
manner,procedure,method	uslūb	أسلوب
manpower workers	al quwwa al bashariya	القوة البشرية
marble	ruḵām	رخام
marketing,sale and purchase	bai' wa shira'	بيع و شراء
marriage	ziwāj	زواج
married person	mutazawwaj	متزوج
martyr	shahid	شـــهيد
master, professor	ustāḏ	أسـتاذ
master of Arts (M.A.)	ustāḏ funūn	أستاذ فنون
material, substance	mādda	مادة
mathematics	riyāḍiyāt	رياضيات
matter, problem, case	mas'ala	مسئلة

mature, legally major	bāliḡ	بالغ
may be, perhaps	rubbamā	رُبّما
meal, food	ṭa'ām	طعام
meaning, sense	ma'na	معنى
means, medium	wasīla	وسيلة
measurement, guage	miqyās	مقياس
medical	ṭibbi	طبي
member, limb	'uḍu	عضو
menstruation	ḥaiḍ	حيض
mental, intellectual	ḏihnī	ذهني
merchant, trader	tājir	تاجر
minor, under age	qāṣir	قاصر
minute (time unit),	daqīqa	دقيقة
misappropriation embezzlement	iḵtilās	إختلاس
miscellaneous,various	mutanawwi'	متنوع
miserable, wretched	bāi's	بائس
misfortune, calamity	muṣība	مصيبة
miss (unmarried womaṇ)	ānisa	آنسة
mister (Mr.)	sayyid	سيد
mix, mingle	mazaja	مزج
mobile	mutaḥarrik	متحرك

moderate,proportionate	mu'tadil	معتدل
modern, new	jadīd	جديد
modify, to change	'addala	عـدّل
money, wealth	māl	مال
money changer	ṣarrāf	صرّاف
mood, frame of mind	mizāj	مـزاج
moral, ehtical	akḻāqi	أخلاقـي
mortgaging, pledge	rahn	رهـن
motion, action	ḥaraka	حركة
motive,cause,reason	bā'iṯ	باعث
municipality,township	baladiya	بلدية
murder, to kill	qatala	قتـل
music	mūsīqā	موسيقي
muslim	muslim	مسلم
must, necessray	lā budd	لا بد
mutual	mutabādil	متبادل
myself	bi-nafsī	بنفسي
mysterious, hidden	ḡāmiḍ	غامض

N

nail	mismār	مسمار
naked, undressed	'uryān	عريان

name	ism	إسم
narrow, tight	ḍīq	ضيق
nation, people	qaum	قوم
nationality,citizenship	jinsiya	جنسية
natural, inborn	ṭabi'ī	طبيعي
nature,natural disposition	ṭabī'a	طبيعة
naval, marine	baḥri	بحري
navigation, shipping	milaḥa	ملاحة
near, close to	qarīb	قريب
necessary,requisite	ḍarūri	ضروري
need, requirement	ḥāja	حاجة
needle, pin	ibra	إبرة
needless,unnecessary	ḡair ḍarūri	غير ضروري
negative, passive	salbi	سلبي
neglect,carelessness	ihmāl	إهمال
negotiation, talk	mufāwaḍa	مفاوضة
neighbour	jār	جار
nervous, nerved	'aṣabī	عصبي
net, network	shabaka	شبكة
never, not at all	abada	أبدا
new, modern	jadīd	جديد

news, message	aḵbār	أخبـار
next, after that	ba'da	بعـد
nice, delicious	laḏīḏ	لذيذ
no	lā	لا
noble, sublime	nabīl	نبيل
nobody	lā aḥad	لا أحد
nomad, rural	badawī	بدوي
non-professional	ḡair fannī	غير فني
nonsense,unintelligible	ḡair ma'qūl	غير معقول
normal, ordinary	'ādī	عادي
notable, famous	shahīr	شهير
note,reminder,report	muḏakkira	مذكرة
nothing	lā shai'	لاشيء
notice, announcement	i'lān	إعلان
nourishment, food	ḡiḏā'	غذاء
number, quantity	'adad	عـدد
nurse (male)	mumarriḍ	ممرض
nurse (female)	mumarriḍa	ممرضة

O

oath, swear	qasam	قسم

obedient	muṭi'	مطيع
object, aim, purpose	ḡāya	غاية
objection, hindrance	māni'	مانع
observe, to see	shāhada	شاهد
obstinate, stubborn	'anīd	عنيد
obstruction, screen	ḥājiz	حاجز
obtain, to get	nāla	نال
occasion, in this connection	fi munāsaba	في مناسبة
odour, smell	rā'iḥa	رائحة
offence, harm, insult`	aḏan	أذي
offer,presentation	'arḍ	عرض
office, agency	maktab	مكتب
officer, employee	muwaẓẓaf	موظف
office boy	farrāsh	فراش
old, noble	'atīq	عتيق
omission, neglect	iḡfāl	إغفال
on, top, at, by	'alā	علي
only, no more	faqaṭ	فقط
open, to switch on	fataḥa	فتح
operate, to employ, make work	ishtaḡala	إشتغل

opinion, idea	fikr	فكر
opportunity, chance	furṣa	فرصة
oppose, to resist	'ataraḍa	اعترض
opposite, contrast	ḍidd	ضد
option, selection	ik̲tiyār	إختيار
oral, orally	shafawī	شفوي
organ, limb, member	'uḍw	عضو
organisation	munaẓẓama	منظمة
orient, the east	al-sharq	الشرق
original,authentic,pure	aṣli	أصلي
other, one more	āk̲ar	آخر
outlook	maẓhar	مظهر
outward, external	k̲āriji	خارجي
overcoat	m'ataf	معطف
overseer, supervisor	murāqib	مراقب
overtime,additional payment	ajar iḍāfi	أجر إضافي
own property	milk k̲ās	ملك خاص
owner, proprietor,holder	mālik	مالك

P

package,parcel,bundle	razma	رزمة

pact, agreement	mu'āhada	معاهدة
page, surface, sheet	ṣafḥa	صفحة
pain, suffering, ache	alam	ألم
painter	dahhān	دهان
paper, paper money	waraq	ورق
pardon, excuse me	'afwan	عفوا
part, portion, section	juz'	جزء
participate, become partner	shāraka	شارك
particular, personal, private	ḵuṣūṣi	خصوصي
particulars, details	tafāṣīl	تفاصيل
partition,division,splitting	taqsīm	تقسيم
partner, associate, co-owner	sharīk	شريك
party,group,community	jamā'a	جماعة
passage,method,route	ṭarīq	طريق
past	māḍin	ماض
paste, cream	ma'jūn	معجون
patience, firmness self control	ṣabr	صبر
patron, client,customer	zabūn	زبون
pattern, model	namuḏaj	نموذج

pauper, poor	faqīr	فقير
pavement,platform	raṣīf	رصيف
pay, to push	dafa'a	دفع
peace	salām	سلام
peasant, farmer	fallāḥ	فلاح
pen	qalam	قلم
pending, delayed	mu'ajjal	مؤجل
pensioner, retired	mutaqā'id	متقاعد
peon, domestic servant	k̲ādim	خادم
perfect, complete	kāmil	كامل
perfume, scent	'iṭrīya	عطرية
peril, risky, danger	k̲aṭir	خطر
period, role, phase	daur	دور
permanent, durable	dā'im	دائم
permission,authorisation	id̲n	إذن
permit, licence	ruk̲ṣa	رخصة
person, individual, some body	shak̲ṣ	شخص
petition, demand, application	ṭalab	طلب
petitioner, applicant	muqaddim al-ṭalab	مقدم الطلب
pharmacy, drug store	ṣaidalīya	صيدلية

pickle	ṭurshi	طرشي
picture, copy, duplicate	ṣūra	صورة
pilgrim to Mecca	ḥājj	حاج
pilot	tayyar	طيّار
pin	dabbūs	دبوس
pink, rose coloured	wardī	وردي
pit, hole	ḥufra	حفرة
place, location, site	makān	مكان
plain, simple	sahl	سهل
plants, vegetation	nabāt	نبات
player, sportsman	lā'ib	لاعب
please, will you please	min faḍlak	من فضلك
plumber, smelter	sabbāk	سباك
pocket, purse	jaib	جيب
point, dot, spot	nuqta	نقطة
policeman, officer	shurṭī	شرطي
policy, politics	siyasa	سياسة
polite, well-mannered	mu'addab	مؤدب
pollution,dirty,filthy	najis	نجس
population,inhabitants	sukkān	سكان
port, harbour	minā´	ميناء

position, situation	ḥāla	حالـة
positive,affirmative	ijābi	ايجابي
possible	mumkin	ممكـــن
post-mortem,anatomy	tashrīḥ	تشريح
pour, fill, cast	ṣabba	صبّ
power,ability,energy	ṭāqa	طاقـة
practically,applied	'amali	عملي
practice of some profession	muzāwala	مزاولة
prayer, blessing	ṣalāh	صلوة
precious, valuable	ṯamīn	ثمـين
preference,priority	tafḍīl	تفضيل
pregnant,holding,carrying	ḥāmil	حامل
premises,place of stay	manzil	منزل
preparation, arranging, drafting	i'dād	إعداد
prepared, ready	musta'idd	مستعد
prescription of doctor	rushīta	رشيتة
present,attending, prepared	ḥāḍir	حاضر
preservation, protection	ḥifẓ	حفظ
pressure, to oppress,	ḍaḡaṭa	ضغط

pretty, beautiful	jamīl	جميل
prevail, to dominate	ḡalaba	غلب
price, exchange rate	si'r	سعر
prince, leader	amīr	أمير
principal, dean, chief	'amīd	عميد
printing press	maṭba'	مطبع
printed material	maṭbu'	مطبوع
prison, jail	sijn	سجن
privilage,honour	imtiyāz	إمتياز
problem, difficulty	mushkila	مشكلة
proceedings, to take measures	ittak̲ad̲a ijrā'āt	اتخذ إجراءات
proclamation,declaration	i'lān	إعلان
procure, to obtain	ḥaṣala 'alā	حصل علي
produce, to make	antaja	أنتج
production,manufacture	intāj	إنتاج
profession,job,trade	mihna	مهنة
professor, teacher	ustād̲	استاذ
profit,gain,advantage	naf'	نفع
programme,plan, schedule	barnāmaj	برنامج
progress,advance, lead	taqaddum	تقدم

promise, to give one's word	wa'ada	وعد
promotion, encouragement	al-ruqīy	الرقي
prompt,speedy,rapid	sarī'	سريع
pronounce,to talk	naṭaqa	نطق
proof,evidence	burhān	برهان
propoganda	di'āya	دعاية
property,ownership	milkīya	ملكية
proportional,interrelation	tanāsub	تناسب
proposal,to suggest	iqtaraha	إقترح
prospectus,circular;order	manshūr	منشور
prosperity,success	falah	فلاح
protection,patronage	ḥimāya	حماية
provide,to make ready	jahaza	جهز
province, area, region	iqlīm	إقليم
pull, to draw	jarra	جرّ
pump	ṭulumba	طلمبة
punishment,penalty	'uqūba	عقوبة
pruging,diarrhea	ishāl	إسهال
purpose, intention	qaṣd	قصد
purse,bag,sack	kīs	كيس

push,drive back	dafa'a	دفع
put, to place, fix	waḍ'	وضع
put on clothes	labisa	لبس
put off fire, fire service	iṭfā'	إطفاء
put up, have patience	ṣabara	صبر
puzzled,confused, stunned	ḥairān	حيران

Q

question	su'āl	سوال
queue, line	ṭabūr	طابور
quotation,loaning	iqtibās	إقتباس

R

rain	maṭar	مطر
raise, to lift, hoist up	rafa'aa	رفع
rank, grade, class	martaba	مرتبة
rare, unusual,precious	nādir	نادر
raw material,crude	ḵām	خام
reading, recital	qirā'a	قراءة
real, actual, genuine	ḥaqīqī	حقيقي
reality, trtue nature	haqīqa	حقيقة

rear part or behind	k̲alf	خلف
reason,mind,intellect	'aql	عقل
receipt of letter/amount	waṣala	وصل
receive,taking over	istilām	استلام
reception, welcome	istiqbāl	إستقبال
reckon, to count	'adda	عدّ
recognition,acceptance	i'tirāf	اعتراف
recommendation, advice, legacy	waṣīya	وصية
record,register,list	sijill	سجلّ
recover,reclamation	istirjā'	استرجاع
reduction, cut back	tak̲fīḍ	تخفيض
reference, competent authority	marāji'	مراجع
refine, purified	muṣaffan	مصفًّى
refreshing,animating	mun'ish	منعش
refreshment, foodstuffs	makūlāt	مأكولات
refrigerator, ice box	t̲allāja	ثلاجة
refusal, rejection	rafḍ	رفض
regards,greetings,salute	tahiya	تحية
regretful, sorry	āsif	آسف
relationship, kinship	qarāba	قرابة

reliance, credit	i'timād	اعتماد
relief,help,aid	najda	نجدة
religion, sect	diyāna	ديانة
remember, to recollect	taḏakkara	تذكّر
remote, far away	ba'īd	بعيد
remove,to transport	naqala	نقل
renewal,remodeling	tajdīd	تجديد
rent, hire, charge	ujra	أجرة
repair,improvement	iṣlāh	اصلاح
reply to letter, answer	jawāb	جواب
report,account,decision	taqrīr	تقرير
represent, to deputise	nāba 'an	ناب عن
representative, delegate, deputy	mandub	مندوب
republic	jumhūrīya	جمهورية
resolve, to decide	qarrara	قرّر
respect, honouring	iḥtiram	إحترام
responsibility	mas'ūliya	مسئولية
rest,leisure,comfort	rāḥa	راحة
restrict, to block	ḥaṣar	حصر
retirement,resignation	istiqāla	استقالة
return, to come back	'auda	عودة

revolver	musaddas	مسدّس
reward, prize	jā'iza	جائزة
rich, prosperous	ḡaniy	غني
rival, competitor	munāfis	منافس
rob, to steal	salaba	سلب
rough,coarse,harsh	k̲ashin	خشن
round, circle, extent	dā'ira	دائرة
rubber, elastic	maṭṭat	مطّاط
ruin, to destroy	k̲araba	خرب
rule, law, regulation	qānūn	قانون
run, to rush	rakaḍa	ركض

S

sacred, holy	muqaddas	مقـــدس
safe, faultless, unhurt	sālim	سالم
safety, security, peace	amn	أمن
salary, pay	rātib	راتـب
sale	bai'	بيع
salesman, dealer	bā'i'	بائع
sample,pattern,form	namuḏaj	نموذج
sanction,approval	qubūl	قبول

sand	raml	رمل
sanitary,hygenic	ṣiḥḥi	صحّي
satiated, satisfied	shab'ān	شبعان
saving food, provision	d̲ak̲īra	ذخيرة
say, to tell	qāla	قال
scavenger,sweeper	kannās	كناس
school,secondary etc.	madrasa	مدرسة
science,knowledge	'ilm	علم
scientist,scholar,learned	'alim	عالم
scissors	miqaṣṣ	مقص
searching,investigation	taftīsh	تفتيش
secretly, privately	sirran	سرّا
secretary	kātib al-sirr	كاتب السر
section,department,class	qism	قسم
secure, reliable	ma'mūm	مأمون
security,guaranty,surety	ḍamān	ضمان
seizure, arrest	qabḍ	قبض
send letter or forward	arsala	أرسل
sense,consciousness	shu'ur	شعور
separate, to divide	farraqa	فرّق
serious, important	muhim	مهم

servant, employee	k̲ādim	خادم
service, occupation	k̲idma	خدمة
set, group, collection	majmū'a	مجموعة
settle, to stay, remain	istaqarra	استقرّ
settlement, adjustment	taswiya	تسوية
several, numerous	muta'adid	متعدد
sex, gender, category	jins	جنس
shadow, protection	ẓill	ظل
shake a thing	hazza	هزّ
shape, form, figure	shakl	شكل
shaping, formation	tashkīl	تشكيل
she	hiya	هي
shirt, dress, gown	qamīṣ	قميص
shoe, sandal	ḥid̲a'	حذاء
shop, store	dukkān	دكّان
short, small	qaṣīr	قصير
shortage, to reduce	naqaṣa	نقص
show room, exhibition	ma'riḍ	معرض
shut, to lock, close	ḡalaqa	غلق
sign,signal,hint	ishāra	إشارة
silence	ṣamt	صمت

silk	ḥarīr	حرير
silver	fiḍḍa	فضة
sink, be drowned	ḡariqa	غرق
sit down	jalasa	جلس
size, bulk	ḥajm	حجم
sleep, to go to bed	nāma	نام
smell, to breathe	shamma	شمّ
smile	ibtisām	إبتسام
smoking tobacco	tadkīn	تدخين
soap	ṣābūn	صابون
social,community,group	ijtimā'i	اجتماعي
soft, gentle, mild	līn	لين
solar	shamsī	شمسي
solitary,single,isolated	wāḥid	واحد
solution of a problem	ḥall	حل
something, a thing	shai'	شيء
sometimes	aḥyānan	أحيانا
song, melody	uḡniya	أغنية
soul, spirit	rūḥ	روح
sound, voice, tune	ṣaut	صوت
sour, acid	ḥāmiḍ	حامض

source, point of origin	maṣdar	مصـدر
sparkling, shining	lāmi'	لامع
speak, to converse	takallama	تكلم
specialist in medicine	ik̲ṣā'i	إخصـائي
specialization in science or arts	tak̲aṣṣus	تخصص
specific, fixed	mu'ayyan	معين
specification, detailed description	muwāṣafāt	مواصفات
spectacles, telescope, eye glasses	naẓẓāra	نظّارة
spend money	anfaqa	أنفق
spontaneously, automatically	tilqāi'yan	تلقائيا
spread, to extend	madda	مدّ
spy	jāsūs	جاسوس
stand up, to rise	qāma	قام
start, to begin	shara'a	شرع
statement,declaration	bayān	بيان
station, stopping place	maḥaṭṭa	محطة
stationary, paper	qirṭās	قرطـاس
stay, residence permit	iqāma	إقامة
steel, solid	ṣulb	صلب

stiff, motionless	jāmid	جـامد
stir, to move, propel	harraka	حرّك
stone	ḥajar	حجر
storm, violent wind	'āṣifa	عاصفة
story, tale	qiṣṣa	قصة
stove, fire place	mauqid	موقد
straight, righteous	mustaqim	مستقيم
stranger, foreigner	ajnabi	أجنبي
strength,power,potency	quwwa	قوة
strike, to hit	ḍaraba	ضـــرب
stroke,upset,jolt	ṣadma	صدمة
strong, forceful	qawiiya	قوية
struggle, dispute	nidāl	نضال
student, applicant	tālib	طالب
study	dirāsa	دراسـة
stupid, foolish	aḥmaq	أحمق
successful	nājiḥ	ناجح
sufficient, adequate	kāfin	كافٍ
superb, valuable	nafīs	نفيس
supply a thing, to provide	zawwada	زوّد
surely, certainly	yaqīnan	يقينا

surface, plane,terrace	saṭḥ	سطح
surprising,astonishing	'ajīb	عجيب
survival,remaining	baqā'	بقاء
suspect, to doubt	shakka	شكّ
suspend, to be without work	'aṭṭila	عطّل
swallow, to gulp	bala'a	بلع
sweet, nice, pleasant	ḥulw	حلو
swimming	sibāḥa	سباحة
symbol, pin code	ramz	رمز
sympathy, compassion	in'iṭāf	إنعطاف
synagogue	alkanīs	الكنيس

T

table, desk, rack	minḍada	منضدة
tailor	k̲ayyāṭ	خياط
take,to receive	ak̲ad̲a	أخذ
talent, intelligence	d̲aka'	ذكاء
tall, high, long	ṭawīl	طويل
tannery	madbaḡa	مدبغة
tape, ribbon, band	sharīṭ	شريط
tax, duty, levy	ḍarīb	ضريبة

team, band, party	farīq	فريق
tedious, dull	mut'ib	متعب
temperature	darajat al ḥarara	درجة الحرارة
temple	ma'bad	معبد
temporarily	muwaqqatan	مؤقّتا
tent, pavilion	ḵaima	خيمة
terms, conditions	shrūṭ	شروط
test, trial	iḵtibār	إختبار
text, wording	naṣṣ	نص
thanks, gratitude	shukr	شكر
that	ḏālika	ذلك
they	hum	هم
thick	samīk	سميك
thief, robber	liṣṣ	لصّ
thin, light weight	ḵafīf	خفيف
thirsty	'aṭshān	عطشان
this, herewith	hāḏā	هذا
thought, idea, concept	fikra	فكرة
thread, cord, fiber	ḵaiṭ	خيط
through, by means of	biwasiṭa	بواسطة
ticket, note	taḏkira	تذكرة

tie, bandage	ribāṭ	رباط
tight, scarce	ḍayyiq	ضيق
tin, can, container	tanaka	تنكـة
tobacco	tibḡ	تبغ
tools, instruments	adawāt	أدوات
torch	mash 'al	مشعل
touch, feel withhand	lamasa	لمس
tourists, traveler	suwwāḥ	سواح
tower	burj	برج
traditional,customary	taqlīdī	تقليـدي
traffic police	shurṭat al murūr	شرطة المرور
training, coaching	tadrīb	تدريب
translation,interpretation	tarjama	ترجمة
translator,interpreter	mutarjim	مترجم
tree, shrub, bush	shajara	شـجرة
trail,practice,experiment	tajriba	تجربة
turn, fold up, to wrap	laffa	لـفّ

U

ugly, disgraceful	qabīḥ	قبيح
unable	ḡair qādir	غير قادر

unacceptable	ḡair maqbūl	غير مقبول
uncomfortable	ḡair murīḥ	غير مريح
unconscious, careless	ḡāfil	غافل
under, below	taḥtu	تحت
undoubtedly	bilā raib	بلا ريب
unfinished, incomplete	ḡair mukammal	غير مكمل
unfit, improper	ḡair munāsib	غير مناسب
union, harmony, unity	ittiḥād	اتحاد
unit, single group	waḥda	وحدة
unknown things	majhūl	مجهول
unmarried, bachelor	a'zab	أعزب
unnecessary	ḡair lāzim	غير لازم
unofficial	ḡair rasmi	غير رسمي
unprepared, not ready	ḡair musta'id	غير مستعد
unreasonable,illogical	ḡair m'aq ūl	غير معقول
unusual, abnormal	ḡair 'adi	غير عادي
up, upstairs, on top	fauqa	فوق
use, to utilize	ista'mala	استعمل
useless, false, invalid	bāṭil	باطل

V

vacancies	shāwaḡir	شواغر
vacation, holiday	'uṭla	عطلة
valid, proper, good	ṣaliḥ	صالح
(invalid, useless)	ḡair ṣaliḥ	غير صالح
validity, usefulness	ṣalāḥiya	صلاحية
valuable, worthy	ḏu qīma	ذو قيمة
veil, woman's veil	ḥijāb	حجاب
veterinarian	ṭabib baiṭari	طبيب بيطري
view, sight, out look	manzar	منظر
virgin	bākira	باكرة
visa	tashīra	تأشيرة
visa for transit	tashirat murūr	تأشيرة مرور
vital, essential to life	ḥayawī	حيوي
void, not busy, vacant	furrāḡ	فراغ
violation, contradiction	muḵālafa	مخالفة

W

wages, pay, rate, fee	ajar	أجر
waited, expected	intaẓara	انتظر
waiting,expectation	intiẓār	انتظار

walk, going	mashy	مشي
wander, to move about	ṭāfa	طاف
warm, hot, zealous	ḥārr	حار
was, to be, take place	kāna	كان
wash, to launder	ḡasala	غسـل
waste, extravagance	isrāf	إسـراف
watchman, vigilant,	ḥāris	حارس
weak, feeble	ḍa'īf	ضعيف
weave, to knit	nasaja	نسج
wedding reception	ḥaflat al 'urs	حفلة العرس
weight, measure	wazn	وزن
welder, solderer	laḥḥam	لحام
what	māḏā - mā	ماذا/ما
wheel, bicycle	'ajla	عجلـة
when, at what time	matā	متى
where	aina	أين
whether, if, whenever	iḏa	إذا
white, bright, clean	abyaḍ	أبيض
who, whoever	man	من
why, for what reason	li-māḏa	لماذا
widow	armala	أرملة

widower	armal	أرمل
wild, uncivilized	waḥshi	وحشي
will, wish, will power	irāda	إرادة
wing, part of building	janāḥ	جناح
wire	silkī	سلكي
wireless,radio message	lā-silkī	لا سلكي
wisdom, philosophy	ḥikma	حكمة
wiseman, physician	ḥakīm	حكيم
with, accompanied by	ma'a	مع
without, excluding	bi-duni	بدون
woman, wife	imra'a	إمرأة
womb, uterus, kinship	riḥm	رحم
wood, timber	k̲ashb	خشب
word, speech	kalima	كلمة
workshop, repair shop	warsha	ورشة
worthy, deserving	mustaḥiqq	مستحق
write, he wrote	kataba	كتب

Y

yes, indeed, surely	na'am	نعم
you (m)	anta	أنت

you (f)	anti	أنت
youngman, youth	shabb	شاب
yourself	nafsak	نفسك

Z

zeal, enthusiasm	ḥamās	حماس
zero, nothig	ṣifr	صفر